1000 GREAT MOVIE MOMENTS

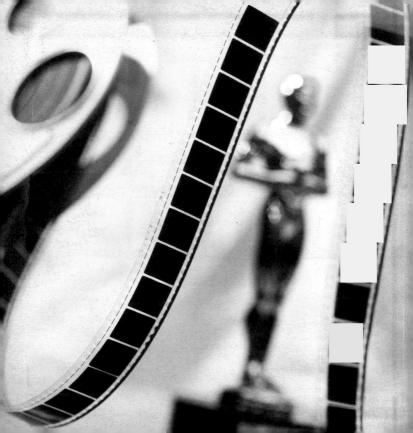

1000 GREAT MOVIE MOMENTS

DAVID BAIRD

MQP

Published by MQ Publications Limited

12 The Ivories, 6–8 Northampton Street, London, N1 2HY

email: mail@mqpublications.com

website: www.mqpublications.com

Copyright © 2004 MQ Publications Limited

Text copyright © 2004 David Baird

Editor: Tracy Hopkins

Editorial Assistant: Céline Hughes

Designer: Philippa Jarvis

ISBN: 1-84072-483-8

10 9 8 7 6 5 4 3 2 1

Printed and bound in Italy

We would like to acknowledge the many talented screenwriters whose
words have enriched this book. Thank you for providing generations
of movie-goers with so many unforgettable pieces of dialogue.

Picture Credits: p.2: © Royalty-Free/CORBIS; p.8, p.30, p.54, p.260, p.284, p.328:
© Bettmann/CORBIS; p.76, p.100, p.168, p.192, p.214, p.306, p.350, p.392, p.414,
p.434: © John Springer Collection/CORBIS; p.122: © SUNSET BOULEVARD/CORBIS
SYGMA; p.146, p.238, p.370: © Underwood & Underwood/CORBIS.

Contents

Introduction

What constitutes a great movie moment, and why do some scenes resonate so effectively and unforgettably with every new generation that encounters them? There are as many answers to these questions as there are wonderful movies, and there is no single rule that will guarantee a phenomenal moment. A scene may be memorable because it contains spectacular visual images or effects, a significant plot development, revelation, or piece of dialogue; or simply because it is exceptionally funny, scary, romantic, shocking, or dramatic.

This book is a celebration of moments from more than a hundred years of movies. Each entry is capable of triggering memories of the film it comes from, or, if you haven't seen the film, of inspiring you to do so. Just say the word "Rosebud" to any film fan, and the entire influential epic *Citizen Kane* is instantly recalled; or perhaps remark, "There's no place like home" and we are all transported into the magical world of *The Wizard of Oz*.

Countless films deserve a place in this book, and many of these contain several legendary moments that merit mention. There will, no doubt, be some omissions, but I hope there will also be some pleasant and thought-provoking surprises. Some moments have been chosen to encourage debate, or even argument, as each of us will have our favorites and our own ideas of what makes a film scene great.

There are a thousand moments here to fuel the imagination and I'm sure that they will stimulate your own thoughts of a thousand more. Charlie Chaplin once famously declared, "Movies are a fad," but the test of time has certainly proved him wrong.

Action &
Adventure

Action and adventure films are spectacular and energetic events that offer us exciting stories, new experiences, exotic locations, and resourceful heroes struggling against incredible odds. They are often great box-office hits created with pure audience escapism in mind, but they can still contain incredible cinematic moments. These movies are laced with explorations, discoveries, battles, disasters, and often a glimpse at real history. They each have their own rhythm and style, but experiencing the dynamics of any of these movies is like riding a roller coaster that leaves you glad to reach the end, but longing to come back for more.

Previous page: Humphrey Bogart and Katharine Hepburn in *The African Queen* (1951).

1 What kind of man would defy a king?

Legendary Scottish hero William Wallace and his clan of followers turn their backs on the invading English forces, raise their kilts, and show them their backsides; "They may take our lives, but they'll never take our FREEEEEDOM!"

BRAVEHEART, 1995

2 Only the rainbow can duplicate its brilliance!

Errol Flynn as Robin Hood has a classic, thrilling sword duel with Basil Rathbone as Sir Guy of Gisbourne on a winding stone staircase in the epic film's finale.

THE ADVENTURES OF ROBIN HOOD, 1938

3 A glorious saga

American POW Virgil "The Cooler King" Hilts sits in solitary confinement, endlessly bouncing a baseball against a wall, catching it in his mitt—and driving the goons crazy.

THE GREAT ESCAPE, 1963

4 Fortune and glory!

Archaeologist Indiana Jones is deep inside a concealed temple. He produces a small drawstring bag filled with sand, estimates the weight of the small gold artifact in front of him, and deftly replaces the artifact with the bag to avoid triggering any booby traps. But then the rumbling starts. The walls start to collapse, and Jones runs, narrowly avoiding poisonous darts and arrows. He then turns and sees a huge boulder rolling in his direction...

RAIDERS OF THE LOST ARK, 1981

5 Romance soaring above the Andes! Drama thundering across a continent!

The camera keeps us in the control room, so we can only hear Joe's radio responses and the drone of his plane's engine as he attempts to land in the fog. Geoff tries to talk him down three times, until we finally hear Joe over the radio: "Give me one more chance. I think I see a hole. Yeah, I do see one. I'm comin' down, Geoff...It's all right, Geoff, I see the lights. I'll make it easy."

ONLY ANGELS HAVE WINGS, 1939

6 "The air! Isn't it wonderful!"

Exhausted and resigned to dying with Charlie aboard their grounded boat, Rosie prays, "Dear Lord, we've come to the end of our journey...I pray to You to be merciful...open the doors of heaven for Charlie and me." The camera shows us that they are only yards away from the lake they seek. The night's rain swells the river, raises the *African Queen* from the hold of the reeds, and carries them onto the lake.

THE AFRICAN QUEEN, 1951

7 Nobody else would have dared it because nobody else would have the nerve! Just Danny Ocean and his 11 pals—the crazy night they blew all the lights in Las Vegas!

The Rat Pack boys play old army buddies who have successfully robbed five Las Vegas casinos. The money is stashed in the coffin of a dead friend, and they're at the funeral hoping to retrieve it when they discover to their horror and disbelief that their loot is being cremated before their eyes.

OCEAN'S 11, 1960

8 All hands...

A remarkable scene, taken from real life, shows an armada of small civilian boats sailing from England in an epic bid to rescue thousands of Allied troops trapped on the beaches of Dunkirk.

DUNKIRK, 1958

9 Quintessentially British

The scene that shall always remain with me is that of Mrs. Miniver (unforgettably played by the beautiful Greer Garson) in a bomb shelter, reading *Alice in Wonderland* to her children during a terrifying Nazi air raid.

MRS. MINIVER, 1942

10 Long live adventure...and adventurers!

When the natives realize that "would-be king" Sean Connery is only human, they chase him onto a flimsy rope bridge suspended over a vast ravine. Connery breaks into a hymn, which is accompanied by "brother" Michael Caine, as the natives cut the ropes and send Connery plunging to his death.

THE MAN WHO WOULD BE KING, 1975

11 God bless our ships and all who sail in them

Captain Kinross (Noel Coward) of the sunken destroyer
HMS *Torrin* delivers a final emotional address to his stalwart
but depleted crew honoring their lost vessel and shipmates:
"If they had to die, what a grand way to go!"

IN WHICH WE SERVE, 1942

12 Vietnam can kill me but it can't make me care

This movie is full of fine moments, but perhaps the most
poignant is the scene of the surviving troop members
singing *The Mickey Mouse Club* theme song as they pass
by the burning buildings and scenes of carnage.

FULL METAL JACKET, 1987

13 Hold the ice...

The most stunning and realistic sequence ever filmed was both
completely real and extremely dangerous. It's the scene of Anna
Moore's (Lillian Gish) daring, last-second rescue from a moving
ice floe before going over a waterfall.

WAY DOWN EAST, 1920

14 Who is Lara Croft?

After parachuting from a plane in her Land Rover, Lara Croft drives through the jungle to an ancient temple. She follows a mysterious girl to a place where unique jasmine grows, and she picks a flower. Then, suddenly, the ground gives way beneath her.

LARA CROFT: TOMB RAIDER, 2001

15 From a place you've never heard of comes a story you'll never forget

It's nail-biting stuff as the young Australian soldiers (including Mel Gibson) begin their final suicidal bayonet charge against the impenetrable Turkish trenches just moments before altered orders arrive…

GALLIPOLI, 1981

16 "Pardon me, your teeth are in my neck."

At an elegant ball, numerous vampires dance a minuet with the three disguised human interlopers hidden among them. The dancers turn and head toward the great mirrored wall and, of course, vampires have no reflection…

THE FEARLESS VAMPIRE KILLERS, 1967

17 If only...

There is a particularly exhilarating sequence in which big-game hunter Captain Thorndike gets to within an easy shooting distance of Hitler's summer palace in the Bavarian Alps. He aims directly at the dictator's head and pulls the trigger—but there is no cartridge in the gun.

MAN HUNT, 1941

18 Collide with destiny

After the gargantuan vessel finally slips into the deep, Jack is in the dark, silent, and freezing water, clinging onto the piece of debris that his true love is lying on top of:

Rose: "I love you, Jack."

Jack: "Don't you do that, don't say your good-byes..."

TITANIC, 1997

19 Tale of a sea horse

In a beautifully photographed scene, the young Alec Ramsey and a black Arabian stallion bond with each other on a deserted beach after surviving a shipwreck.

THE BLACK STALLION, 1979

20 Checkmate

The world-weary knight makes his confession to a hooded priest, who, unbeknownst to him, is actually Death. After a wonderful speech about the futility of life and the yearning for proof of God's existence, the knight foolishly confesses that he is buying time by playing chess with Death. At that moment, Death finally reveals himself: "I'll remember that!"

THE SEVENTH SEAL, 1957

21 The love of brother for brother is steadfast as the stars...

The three young Geste brothers are playing at their English home. They perform a mock Viking funeral by placing a toy dog at the feet of a "dead" toy sailor in a model ship, which they set afire and let float away on the pond. "That's what I want when my turn comes. I'd give anything to have a Viking's funeral with a dog at my feet and the last post blown for me, if it weren't too much trouble."

BEAU GESTE, 1939

22 Following orders isn't the only way to become a hero...

In one scene, a pilot (Matthew Broderick) and a researcher (Helen Hunt) break into a government lab to rescue chimpanzees being used in the mysterious "Project X."

PROJECT X, 1987

23 Who needs bridges?

James Bond and Scaramanga end up on opposite sides of a river during a car chase. Bond sees a twisted, collapsed bridge and quickly makes a calculation. He speeds toward it and launches his car into the air. The car rolls over, then lands squarely and safely on the other side of the river.

THE MAN WITH THE GOLDEN GUN, 1974

24 Out-leaping the maddest imaginings! Out-thrilling the wildest thrills!

Seven decades after the film's release, the giant ape's final moments on top of New York's Empire State Building still holds immense power, especially when he gently, lovingly releases Fay Wray before plunging to the ground...

KING KONG, 1933

25 You can't take it with you

After his life-or-death fight with Marcus, McTeague is stranded out on the great salt flats. The pathetic figure assesses his situation—a bag of gold on the saddle of the dead donkey, no water, and the body of his old friend still handcuffed to him in the middle of Death Valley.

GREED, 1925

26 Going down...

The greatest dueling scene ever captured on film is that between the Pirate Captain and the Black Pirate, and it includes the spectacular stunt of the Black Pirate stabbing his knife into the ship's sail and riding down it as it tears.

THE BLACK PIRATE, 1926

27 If adventure has a name... it must be Indiana Jones!

Indiana Jones awakes to find himself on a plane, which the pilots have just bailed out of. He sits at the controls and looks around the cockpit, while blonde bombshell Willie watches in a state of panic. "You do know how to fly, don't you?" she asks. "Um, no. Do you?"

INDIANA JONES AND THE TEMPLE OF DOOM, 1984

28 British stiff upper lip

Japanese Colonel Saito memorably voices his opinion of the British prisoners of war, who perplex him, "I hate the British! You are defeated but you have no shame. You are stubborn but you have no pride. You endure but you have no courage. I hate the British!"

THE BRIDGE ON THE RIVER KWAI, 1957

29 Discipline is the thing

The *Bounty* is captained by tyrannical, sadistic disciplinarian Captain William Bligh, who orders the flogging of a dead man to set an example to the rest of the crew. He tells his well-respected first mate Christian, "They respect but one law—the law of fear. I expect you to carry out whatever orders I give, whenever I give them."

MUTINY ON THE BOUNTY, 1935

30 The screen has never come so close to the heart of a man!

It's edge-of-the-seat stuff as James Stewart flies the famous plane solo across the sea, trying to stay awake at the stick, splashing his eyes with water…vision blurring…memory fading in and out…and all the time talking…talking…

THE SPIRIT OF ST. LOUIS, 1957

31 God would have mercy. John Rambo won't!

It looks as though the entire Russian army is standing in front of Rambo and his old friend Colonel Trautman, but when the colonel asks, "What do you say, John?" Rambo doesn't hesitate. He quickly loads his weapons and says, "F*** 'em!"

RAMBO III, 1988

32 1750 to 1!
Always outnumbered! Never outfought!

The British officers of the 41st Regiment of the Bengal Lancers, stationed in northwest India, are captured and tortured by the treacherous Mohammed Khan, who threatens one of them, "We have ways of making men talk."

THE LIVES OF A BENGAL LANCER, 1935

33 It's enormous...

While dueling outside a theater with a man who insulted him, Cyrano de Bergerac (beautifully played by Gérard Depardieu) wittily recites poetic variations on what the insult-maker might have called his oversized nose.

CYRANO DE BERGERAC, 1990

34 Six men and three women against the sea—and each other

An unusual group of survivors of a sunken ship share a lifeboat during World War II. Fashion journalist Tallulah Bankhead puts her initials in lipstick on one lucky guy's chest, then uses her diamond bracelet as bait to try to lure a fish for them all to eat.

LIFEBOAT, 1944

35 Playing for their lives

Three Pennsylvanian brothers-in-arms, Steven (John Savage), Nick (Christopher Walken), and Michael (Robert De Niro) are held captive by the Vietnamese and are forced to play a cruel game of Russian roulette for the amusement of their gambling captors.

THE DEER HUNTER, 1978

36 A man went looking for America and couldn't find it anywhere!

There is something about the sight of three doped-up hippies— Dennis Hopper, Peter Fonda, and Jack Nicholson—riding high-handled choppers cross-country to the sounds of '60s acid-rock 'n' roll that captures the spirit of an entire era.

EASY RIDER, 1969

37

Gable and Lancaster make the seas boil in the battle adventure that hits like a torpedo!

Clark Gable plays a navy captain who is determined to get revenge on the Japanese destroyer that sank his previous submarine. When Burt Lancaster, as his new lieutenant, opts for a nonconfrontational approach, the obsessed captain confronts him, "A fleet boat of the navy, with most of her fighting capability intact! And you'd take her back to Pearl, I don't believe it!"

RUN SILENT, RUN DEEP, 1958

38

"It took more than one man to change my name to Shanghai Lily."

The train to Shanghai is being boarded at Peking railroad station as civil war rages through China. One of the passengers, Reverend Carmichael, complains to a fellow passenger about the type of women traveling on the train: "Well, sir, I suppose every train carries its cargo of sin, but this train is burdened with more than its share!"

SHANGHAI EXPRESS, 1932

39 "You're a better man than I am, Gunga Din!"

The British Army battles against a murderous Indian cult in the late nineteenth century. Regimental water carrier Gunga Din is mortally wounded by a bayonet, but he courageously crawls to the top of a tower and blows a bugle, warning approaching British troops and saving them from ambush. Then a bullet hits him, his playing stops, and he falls from the tower.

GUNGA DIN, 1939

40 The nearer they get to their treasure, the further they get from the law.

The grizzled and garrulous Howard regales the other prospectors with tales of the "devilish" lure of gold and how greed usually takes its toll on treasure seekers: "Not even the threat of miserable death'd keep you from trying to add ten thousand more...Like roulette. One more turn, you know, always one more."

THE TREASURE OF THE SIERRA MADRE, 1948

41 Monkey business

Lord Greystoke, after whom the Tarzan legend is based,
sees the staff at a London museum shoot an escaped ape.
The young man holds the ape tenderly as it dies, and
reveals that this was no ordinary ape: "He was my father!"

**GREYSTOKE: THE LEGEND OF TARZAN,
LORD OF THE APES, 1984**

42 A deadly bowler hat!

After a round of golf, Goldfinger orders his mute manservant
Oddjob to demonstrate his strengths, which he does by
throwing, in a Frisbee-like manner, his steel-rimmed bowler
hat at a marble statue—decapitating it effortlessly.

GOLDFINGER, 1964

43 The man with the hat is back. And this time, he's bringing his dad!

Indiana Jones is caught up in a heaving German crowd, holding his
father's Grail diary in his hand. Suddenly someone is standing in front
of him—Adolph Hitler. Hitler takes the book, autographs it, and returns
it, and then walks away from a shocked, but incredibly relieved Jones.

INDIANA JONES AND THE LAST CRUSADE, 1989

44 There she blows!

Peg-legged Captain Ahab's final encounter with the great white whale is a truly thrilling experience. Tangled in the harpoon ropes, he becomes inseparably bound to the mortally wounded creature.

MOBY DICK, 1956

45 Too close for comfort

Maverick is flying with his new copilot, Merlin, in the spectacular final battle scene. The odds are stacked against them and the enemy MiGs have them in a dangerous position. Maverick starts to slow down, and he tells Merlin, "I'm bringing him in closer." To which the horrified Merlin replies, "You're gonna do *what*?!"

TOP GUN, 1986

46 This is the heroic story of the men on the USS *San Pablo*...

A Chinese man, who helped in the U.S. Navy boat's engine room, is considered a traitor by his people. They capture him and torture him on the beach with the death of a thousand cuts, in full view of the American crew. His pal Steve McQueen grabs a rifle and puts him out of his misery, then throws the rifle into the bay.

THE SAND PEBBLES, 1966

47 Live the roaring drama of men against the sea

After half a dozen ice cream sodas, spoiled 12-year-old Harvey, wanting to throw up, leans too far over the rail of a luxury liner and falls unnoticed into the ocean. He is rescued by a gruff but likeable Portuguese fisherman named Manuel—a dory man on a fishing vessel off the Grand Banks: "Fifteen years I've been a fisherman. First time I ever catch a fish like you."

CAPTAINS COURAGEOUS, 1937

48 He's survived the most hostile and primitive land known to man. Now all he's got to do is make it through a week in New York.

Outback Aussie Mick Dundee and reporter Sue Charlton are threatened by young New York muggers wielding a switchblade knife, but Dundee is not a man who scares easily.

"That's not a knife," he says, as he draws out his extremely large survival blade. "Now *that's* a knife."

CROCODILE DUNDEE, 1986

49 She's a girl from the big city. He's a reckless soldier of fortune. For a fabulous treasure, they share an adventure no one could imagine…or survive.

Our unlikely duo is sent on a sudden and unexpected escape route down a steep and muddy chute that winds its way through the jungle undergrowth to the bottom, where Kathleen Turner lands on her back in a pool of water. Michael Douglas suddenly comes flying in after her and lands headfirst in her lap!

ROMANCING THE STONE, 1984

50 The movie that inspired the world to remember

The most realistic combat movie ever made has a lighter moment when Captain John Miller explains how to disable enemy tanks using a sock: "Cram it with as much Composition B as it can hold, rig up a simple fuse, then coat the whole thing with axle grease. Now when you throw it, it should stick. It's a 'sticky bomb.'" Private Reiben then grumbles, "This is great. Now we have to surrender our socks!"

SAVING PRIVATE RYAN, 1998

Comedy

Comedy is one of the most popular and appealing genres—these movies are created solely to make us laugh. Whether slapstick humor, screwball situations, spoofs, parodies, farce, or black comedy, if done well, these films can have us all rolling in the aisles. Comedies provide light-hearted enjoyment and a momentary escape from our everyday lives, and invite us to share in the universal language of laughter.

Previous page: Mae West and W. C. Fields in *My Little Chickadee* (1940).

51 She's making an impression

Unconventional heiress Susan Vance repeatedly dents straitlaced Dr. David Huxley's car, trying to pull it out from a parking space:
David: "You don't understand, this is my car!"
Susan: "Your golf ball, your running board, your car? Is there anything in the world that doesn't belong to you?"
David: "Yes, thank heavens—you!"
BRINGING UP BABY, 1938

52 "Rebels are we, born to be free, just like the fish in the sea."

Fielding Mellish runs off to a banana republic to impress his political activist girlfriend, but winds up as a Fidel Castro-lookalike freedom fighter leading a guerrilla army fed on take-out grilled cheese sandwiches.
Fielding Mellish: "When is the revolution?"
Esposito: "Six months."
Fielding Mellish: "Six months? I have a rented car!"
BANANAS, 1971

53 Never trust your bookie

Chico Marx, disguised as an ice-cream seller, sells Groucho a stack of racing-tips books at the track, each of which requires yet another book as its cross-reference. "Getta yor Tootsie Frootsie ice-a-cream..."

A DAY AT THE RACES, 1937

54 Getting there is half the fun; being there is all of it.

Peter Sellers plays simple-minded gardener Chance, who only knows the world through what he has seen on television. By a strange twist of fate, he becomes a very unlikely political adviser, counseling the president, "First comes spring and summer, but then we have fall and winter. And then we get spring and summer again."

BEING THERE, 1979

55 There's a storm brewing

Bette Davis delivers a truly memorable line with her tobacco-and-cocktail-stained voice as she sets the stage for the party: "Fasten your seatbelts. It's going to be a bumpy night."

ALL ABOUT EVE, 1950

56 A comedy of remarriage

A large clock signals 8 o'clock outside the Gotham Athletic Club, where pale-skinned Jerry Warriner (Cary Grant) prepares to tan himself under a sunlamp: "I've gotta get a deep Florida tan if it takes all afternoon."

THE AWFUL TRUTH, 1937

57 Self-control in action

Eccentric wheelchair-bound scientist and presidential advisor Dr. Strangelove hilariously beats his uncontrollable mechanical hand into submission when it involuntarily makes a Nazi salute.

DR. STRANGELOVE, OR: HOW I LEARNED TO STOP WORRYING AND LOVE THE BOMB, 1964

58 Mass appeal

Every actor's career has its ups and downs, but the late funnyman Dudley Moore could always be relied upon to raise a smile—especially if he happens to be dressed as a nun, and joins in with all the other nuns on a trampoline!

BEDAZZLED, 1967

59 Is marriage necessary?

Geraldine Jeffers accidentally pricks her husband Tom as she pins a note to the bed quilt saying that she is leaving him. Tom wakes up to see her walking out the door with her suitcase. He tumbles down the stairs after her, wearing only his slippers and a pajama top, and wrapped in the quilt. At the elevator, Geraldine explains her determined decision to leave him, as an elevator full of people catches a glimpse of his naked backside.

THE PALM BEACH STORY, 1942

60 Underage drinking

Terry tries to get a bum to buy him some liquor:
Terry: "Pardon me, sir, but I lost my I.D. in…in a flood, and I'd like to get some Old Harper, hard stuff. Would you mind buying a bottle for me?"
Bum: "Why certainly! I lost my wife, too—her name wasn't Idie though, and it wasn't in a flood…"

AMERICAN GRAFFITI, 1973

61 "All you need to start an asylum is an empty room and the right kind of people."

Two hoboes are exchanging banter at the city dump:
Godfrey: "Mike, I wouldn't worry. Prosperity's just around the corner."
Mike: "Yeah. It's been there a long time. I wish I knew which corner."
Just then, socialite Irene Bullock arrives and offers Godfrey $5 to be her "lost man" in a society scavenger hunt. He accepts and goes with her—a decision that will soon change everybody's lives.

MY MAN GODFREY, 1936

62 "It's real crazy!"

Richard Sherman (Tom Ewell) finds it very difficult to be faithful to his absent wife when his voluptuous blonde neighbor (Marilyn Monroe) makes revelations like this:
The Girl: "Let me just go put something on.
I'll go into the kitchen and get dressed."
Sherman: "The kitchen?"
The Girl: "Yes, when it gets hot like this—
you know what I do? I keep my undies in the icebox."

THE SEVEN YEAR ITCH, 1955

63 A nervous romance

After having sex with Annie (Diane Keaton) for the first time, Alvy Singer (Woody Allen) says, "That was the most fun I've ever had without laughing."

ANNIE HALL, 1977

64 Don't stop for lunch

Charlie Chaplin is at his workstation on an assembly line, holding wrenches in both hands to tighten nuts on a stream of steel plates that are moving along the conveyor belt. He pauses for just a moment—and causes chaos for fellow workers down the line!

MODERN TIMES, 1936

65 Mae West gives a "hot time" to the nation

When Serge Stanieff (Gilbert Roland) is introduced to singer Lady Lou (Mae West) he gallantly kisses her hand and says, "I am delighted. I have heard so much about you." To which she wittily retorts, "Yeah, but you can't prove it."

SHE DONE HIM WRONG, 1933

66 Not too loud! The neighbors are complaining

Bud Baxter tries to chat up Fran Kubelik:

Bud: "I looked up your card in the group insurance file. I know your height, your weight, and your social security number. You had mumps, and you had measles, and you had your appendix out."

Fran: "Don't mention the appendix to the fellows in the office, OK? I wouldn't want 'em to get the wrong idea about how you found out."

THE APARTMENT, 1960

67 Sex sells

Successful comedy director John Sullivan rises to his feet to explain to his studio bosses why he wants to make a serious, socially-aware film.

Sullivan: "I want this picture to be a commentary on modern conditions, stark realism, the problems that confront the average man."

LeBrand: "But with a little sex in it!"

Sullivan: "A little, but I don't want to stress it."

SULLIVAN'S TRAVELS, 1941

(39)

68 "Well, all the jokes can't be good. You've got to expect that once in a while."

Capt. Spaulding: "I used to know a fellow who looked exactly like you by the name of Emanuel Ravelli. Are you his brother?"

Signor Ravelli: "I am Emanuel Ravelli."

Capt. Spaulding: "You're Emanuel Ravelli?"

Signor Ravelli: "I am Emanuel Ravelli."

Capt. Spaulding: "Well, no wonder you look like him. But I still insist there is a resemblance."

ANIMAL CRACKERS, 1930

69 A head for heights

Laurel and Hardy, on their way to deliver the deeds to a goldmine, stop at the local saloon, where a group of cowboys are singing "The Blue Ridge Mountains of Virginia." They join in with the singing and, following a bump to the head, Laurel's unexpectedly deep baritone voice becomes a high, feminine soprano.

WAY OUT WEST, 1937

70 High maintenance

Who could forget Sally Albright (Meg Ryan) ordering lunch in her own very particular way?

Sally: "I'd like the chef salad, please, with the oil and vinegar on the side. And the apple pie à la mode. But I'd like the pie heated, and I don't want the ice cream on top. I want it on the side. And I'd like strawberry instead of vanilla if you have it. If not, then no ice cream, just whipped cream, but only if it's real. If it's out of a can, then nothing."

Waitress: "Not even the pie?"

Sally: "No, just the pie. But then not heated."

WHEN HARRY MET SALLY, 1989

71 The maddest comics of the screen!

Groucho Marx makes a memorable speech when he becomes the new president of Huxley College: "Members of the faculty, faculty members, students of Huxley, and Huxley students—I guess that covers everything. Well, I thought my razor was dull until I heard this speech. And that reminds me of a story that's so dirty I'm ashamed to think of it myself."

HORSE FEATHERS, 1932

72 Quelle surprise!

As Monsieur Hulot explores his sister's futuristic kitchen, he drops a glass jug and it bounces right back into his hands. In disbelief he drops it again, and again it bounces back unbroken. He then tries the same trick with another object, which shatters on impact with the floor.

MON ONCLE, 1958

73 Watch out for the Bogeyman

When Allan Felix's wife leaves him, he starts to see an apparition of his movie idol Humphrey Bogart. His fantasy friend offers him some very simple advice about women: "Dames are simple. I never met one that didn't understand a slap in the mouth or a slug from a forty-five."

PLAY IT AGAIN, SAM, 1972

74 Bluebottle blues

W. C. Fields is trying to order lunch in a café, but everything on the menu seems to be unavailable. He comically mutters, "I don't know why I ever come in here—the flies get the best of everything."

NEVER GIVE A SUCKER AN EVEN BREAK, 1941

75 The movie too hot for words!

Tony Curtis dons stolen men's clothing to woo Marilyn Monroe onboard a yacht. Meanwhile, Jack Lemmon, still in drag, must keep the boat's owner occupied—by dancing the sensual tango with him all night long!

SOME LIKE IT HOT, 1959

76 "It's not only against the law, it's wrong!"

Incognito in a pair of dark sunglasses, drama critic and sworn bachelor Mortimer Brewster stands in line for a marriage license: "I've sneered at every love scene in every play. I've written four million words against marriage. Now I'll be hooked to a minister's daughter."

ARSENIC AND OLD LACE, 1944

77 Lost among the playful rich

Two journalists covering a society wedding try to explore the bride's home:

Liz Imbrie: "What's this room? I've forgotten my compass."

Mike Connor: "I'd say, south-by-southwest, parlor-by-living-room."

THE PHILADELPHIA STORY, 1940

78 "Come on in, I'm only shaving!"

Harold Bissonette's (W. C. Fields) attempts to shave are pure ballet in this classic bathroom sequence. He ducks and dives around his oblivious daughter as she beautifies herself in front of the mirror, and he jumps every time she gargles with her mouthwash. "If you want me to cut my throat, keep that up!" he snaps. She gargles again and he mumbles, "Evidently, you do."

IT'S A GIFT, 1934

79 A sobering thought

Early one morning in a bar, Egbert Sousé (W. C. Fields) is offered a job directing a movie for a percentage of the profits. Before making his decision, Egbert turns to the bartender: "Was I in here last night, and did I spend a twenty-dollar bill?" Bartender: "Yeah." Egbert: "Oh boy, what a load that is off my mind. I thought I'd lost it."

THE BANK DICK, 1940

80 "I'm going to be a lady if it kills me."

Nouveau-riche, former hatcheck girl Kitty Packard chats with celebrated actress Carlotta Vance on their way into dinner—which is served at eight!
Kitty: "The guy said that machinery is going to take the place of every profession."
Carlotta: "Oh, my dear, that's something you need never worry about."

DINNER AT EIGHT, 1933

81 Never mince your words

When outspoken reporter Peter Warne is fired and his story is criticized, he drunkenly shouts at his boss on the phone: "In a pig's eye, you will! Hey, listen, monkey face, when you fired me, you fired the best newshound your filthy scandal sheet ever had….That [story] was [written in] free verse, you gashouse palooka!"

IT HAPPENED ONE NIGHT, 1934

82 It's the hilarious answer to who wears the pants!

Adam Bonner gives his wife Amanda a more-than-playful slap.
Amanda: "It felt not only as though you meant it, but as though you felt you had a right to. I can tell."
Adam: "What've you got back there? Radar equipment?"
ADAM'S RIB, 1949

83 Snakes alive!

Standing outside his stateroom, Charles invites Jean inside…to see his snake! Once inside, it becomes clear that he wants to show her his rare Brazilian snake, Emma, but the creature has escaped from her box. Jean grabs the hem of her skirts and screams when she sees Emma, then runs all the way back to her own cabin, with Charles in pursuit.
THE LADY EVE, 1941

84 Suicide is painless

At an army hospital during the Korean War, "Hawkeye" and his surgical pals give "Painless"—a well-endowed, suicidal dentist who thinks he's "become a fairy"—a fitting last supper before administering a "black capsule." "Painless" then climbs into an open coffin and the others take turns to say their good-byes.

M*A*S*H, 1970

85 True comrades

This picture takes place in Paris, in those wonderful days when a siren was a beautiful brunette and not an alarm. Three strangely dressed Russian men enter a luxurious hotel and look around in awe at the splendid lobby. They debate whether it would be right to stay there or if they should go somewhere cheaper and more ordinary, when one says, "Comrades, why should we lie to each other? It's wonderful!"

NINOTCHKA, 1939

86 With strings attached

Form an orderly line, all fans of those trademark Woody Allen vignettes of flashbacks, memories, and strange mental images of how he sees the world. Get a glimpse of Woody Allen as Virgil Starkwell, playing a cello in a marching band.

TAKE THE MONEY AND RUN, 1969

87 They think he's pixilated!

Eccentric poet Longfellow Deeds (Gary Cooper) arrives wearing a leather jacket, a hat, and a bow tie. A man introduces himself as the senior partner in the law firm of Cedar, Cedar, Cedar, and Budington, and Deeds replies, "Budington must feel like an awful stranger."

MR. DEEDS GOES TO TOWN, 1936

88 A comedy romance in pantomime

An ugly monument to "peace and prosperity" is being unveiled in front of assembled dignitaries in the big city. The cover is dramatically removed from the immense stone statue to reveal a black-clothed little tramp (Charlie Chaplin) lying blissfully asleep in its lap.

CITY LIGHTS, 1931

89 The most gloriously mad lark ever to tickle the ribs of young and old alike!

A young woman checks into a boarding house and discovers that the last tenant left behind some belongings—including a pair of canvas sneakers, which are stuck sole-to-sole. As she pries them apart, her comical expression questions what on earth their wearer had stood in!

MONSIEUR HULOT'S HOLIDAY, 1953

90 Just like two peas in a pot

Stan (Stan Laurel) and Ollie (Oliver Hardy) belong to the oldest all-male fraternity order, the Sons of the Desert. After causing a stir by arriving late, they take part in an oath-taking ceremony.

The Ruler: "Do you all solemnly swear to be present at our 87th Annual Convention in Chicago?"

The Group (thunderously respond in unison): "I do!"

Stan (late): "Me, too!"

SONS OF THE DESERT, 1933

91 Together for the first time

W. C. Fields and Mae West meet on a train: he is Cuthbert J. Twillie, a traveling snake-oil salesman, and she is Flower Belle Lee, a lady of rather relaxed virtues. She has been railroaded out of town, while he's hitched a ride. Twillie is delighted when he discovers the lady's name: "What a euphonious appellation!"

MY LITTLE CHICKADEE, 1940

92 Who ya gonna call?

Who can forget the vintage ambulance, newly revamped as an "Ectomobile," bursting out of the Ghostbusters' headquarters, accompanied by the familiar beat of the movie's theme song?

GHOSTBUSTERS, 1984

93 First-class male

Jacques Tati's enthusiastic mailman takes a letter into a vibrant jazz café, which is teeming with jiving servicemen and local girls. He quietly watches them until his fingers, then his foot, and eventually his whole body abandon themselves to the rhythms of the music. He joins in the dancing, and his mailbag becomes his acrobatic, jiving partner.

L'ÉCOLE DES FACTEURS, 1947

94 Dutiful Dad

This movie follows a very harassed father enduring his only daughter's expensive and lavish wedding. At the engagement party he is advised, "from now on, your only function is to pay the bills."
FATHER OF THE BRIDE, 1950

95 All's well that ends well

After an exhausting and hilarious time in America, Mr. Bean returns to his home in England. He tucks up his teddy bear and settles into bed himself, and the camera pans to his bedroom wall to show the original painting "Whistler's Mother"—complete with the new face he's given it!
BEAN, 1997

96 She lost her reputation— and never missed it!

The barker of a carnival uses dazzling performer Tira (Mae West) to lure men into the show: "Over there, Tira, the beautiful Tira, dancing, singing, marvel of the age, supreme flower of feminine pulchritude, the girl who discovered you don't have to have feet to be a dancer."
I'M NO ANGEL, 1933

97 The king of daredevil comedy

Harold Lloyd's antics on the side of a twelve-story skyscraper give us the most famous comic moment in silent-movie history. Lloyd's predicament goes from bad to worse as he climbs the huge clock face on the tower, until the scene's unforgettable climax, which leaves him dangling over the busy city streets from the minute hand as the clock starts to pull away from the wall.

SAFETY LAST, 1923

98 She learned from him

Hildy mocks her ex-husband Walter for the way he tried to convince her not to go through with their divorce: "A big fat lummox like you—hiring an airplane to write: 'Hildy, don't be hasty, remember my dimple. Walter.' It delayed our divorce twenty minutes while the judge went out to watch it."

HIS GIRL FRIDAY, 1940

99 Does she have what it takes?

A gangster, played by Tom Ewell, gives a washed-up agent an offer he can't refuse: to make his protégée girlfriend a star. Jayne Mansfield memorably displays her obvious assets as the leading lady when she performs a somewhat rigid dance to the strains of Little Richard's "She's Got It" while dressed in a scanty little scarlet number.

THE GIRL CAN'T HELP IT, 1956

100 Woody Allen takes a nostalgic look at the future

Woody Allen is cryogenically frozen in 1973 after going into the hospital for a minor operation. He is defrosted 200 years later by a group of radicals, including Diane Keaton, who remarks, "It's hard to believe that you haven't had sex for 200 years." "Two hundred and four," he replies, "if you count my marriage."

SLEEPER, 1973

Horror

Horror films have one specific duty, and that is to do their utmost to frighten us—to make our hair stand on end, and to cause goose bumps to appear on our skin. Scary movies usually focus on the darkest elements of life—on our most basic fears and primal natures. In the early days of filmmaking, they focused on the story, the implied horror, and a scarily-costumed character. But these days, millions are spent on incredible special effects that take us to the edge of what we can bear, let alone to the edge of our seats!

Previous page: Lon Chaney in *The Phantom of the Opera* (1925).

101 If the ghosts don't get you...Dad will!

Hopeful writer Jack Torrance has been typing away for most of the winter in a remote and empty hotel, but when his wife peeks at his latest work, the pages are filled with the same line typed over and over: "All work and no play makes Jack a dull boy."

THE SHINING, 1980

102 "Is this your wife? What a lovely throat."

The most famous moment of the first-ever Dracula movie must be of the bald, bony-fingered vampire climbing the rickety staircase. Cover your neck!

NOSFERATU, 1922

103 It knows what scares you

A family's cute little daughter begins communicating with "something" in the TV static, and then suddenly claims, "They're here."

POLTERGEIST, 1982

104 Flesh to touch...Flesh to burn! Don't keep the Wicker Man waiting!

In the movie's terrifying climax, Police Sergent Howie is brought face-to-face with a huge wicker man, which is to be his cage as he is burned alive...

Sergeant Howie: "I believe in the life eternal, as promised to us by our Lord, Jesus Christ."

Lord Summerisle: "That is good, for believing what you do, we confer upon you a rare gift, these days—a martyr's death."

THE WICKER MAN, 1973

105 You may not believe in ghosts, but you cannot deny terror.

A parapsychologist takes three students to an eerie old New England house to see if the reports of ghostly phenomena there are true. It seems that they might be, in the scene in which one of the girls holds hands with her friend in the dark. When the lights come back on, her friend is not there!

THE HAUNTING, 1963

106 The days are numbered

Jim awakens from a coma and wanders outside the empty hospital to find London completely deserted in this postapocalyptic movie:

Jim: "I wake up today in hospital. I wake up and I'm hallucinating or…"

Mark: "What's your name?"

Jim: "Jim."

Mark: "I'm Mark. This is Selena. OK, Jim, I've got some bad news…"

28 DAYS LATER, 2002

107 Man is the warmest place to hide

A stray husky dog that arrives at a remote Arctic research base turns out to be a shape-shifting alien, and it starts to pick the scientists off one by one. One member of the team suffers a heart attack and, while being treated by the doctor, he springs a hideous surprise: "If I was an imitation, a perfect imitation, how would you know it was me?"

THE THING, 1982

108 A monster science created—but could not destroy!

In this movie based on Mary Shelley's classic Gothic tale, Frankenstein's monster befriends a little girl by a lake, then throws her in the water and accidentally drowns her, in a scene tinged with horror and tragedy.

FRANKENSTEIN, 1931

109 Hour by hour he gets smaller and smaller!

After coming into contact with a radioactive mist, a man begins to shrink. In his newly diminished form, he enters into a life-or-death battle with a household spider!

THE INCREDIBLE SHRINKING MAN, 1957

110 It's really happening

Rosemary (Mia Farrow) is being ravished by a scaly-skinned, goat-eyed Devil who wants her to have his child. The wide-eyed Rosemary suddenly realizes what is happening. Terrified, she calls out, "This is not a dream!"

ROSEMARY'S BABY, 1968

111 Hilarious horror

In this parody of the classic Hammer Horror films, mad professor Kenneth Williams, who has a penchant for boiling beautiful young women in a bubbling vat, gleefully announces an evening of murderous activity with the cry, "Frying tonight!"

CARRY ON SCREAMING, 1966

112 In heaven everything is fine

Henry lives in a squalid apartment and cares for his mutant baby, whose mother has run off. Creepiness fills the screen as Henry goes mad and people start emerging from behind his radiator.

ERASERHEAD, 1976

113 Seven deadly sins. Seven ways to die.

Serial killer John Doe (Kevin Spacey) murders the undesirables of this world in the style of the seven deadly sins they commit. For gluttony, an obese man is forced to eat and eat until his sides literally split.

SEVEN, 1995

114 Full moon rising...

The Oscar-winning scene in which a young man transforms into a wolf shocks audiences every time.

AN AMERICAN WEREWOLF IN LONDON, 1981

115 She was marked with the curse of those who slink and court and kill by night!

In New York, a woman is being stalked through the park by a sinister, unseen feline presence. All of a sudden, a bus screeches to a halt, its air brakes hissing. This unforgettable "fake scare" still makes audiences jump in their seats.

CAT PEOPLE, 1942

116 A Peck with a pick

There's only one way to kill the evil child Damien (Harvey Stephens) and save the world: his adopted father (Gregory Peck) must stab the little boy through the heart—which is exactly what he's about to do when the police open fire...

THE OMEN, 1976

117 Can a full-grown woman truly love a midget?

A trapeze artist and her strongman lover plot to kill a wealthy midget, but they haven't considered the solidarity of his freak show brethren, who plan to exact a terrible revenge.

FREAKS, 1932

118 A real oddity

Eccentric professor Michael Hordern, who is on vacation in Norfolk, England, awakes one night to see the sheets on the spare bed in the room stiffen and move, as if possessed by a spirit.

WHISTLE AND I'LL COME TO YOU, 1968

119 A masterpiece of horror that shocked cinema for decades!

In the most moving and shocking moment of this classic horror movie, the young woman removes the phantom's mask to reveal his deformed face. "Feast your eyes!" he exclaims. "Glut your soul on my accursed ugliness!"

THE PHANTOM OF THE OPERA, 1925

120 The monster created by atoms gone wild

Compassion blends with suspense when scientist Andre Delambre creates a new teleportation device in his basement laboratory. After a few test runs, Delambre decides to experiment on himself. He steps into the cubicle, completely unaware that a small housefly has followed him, and disintegrates. When Delambre rematerializes, he insists on keeping his head and arm covered, for something went terribly wrong with the experiment...

THE FLY, 1958

121 Everything you've heard is true

Film footage, shot by three missing students, is discovered, and we quickly realize that they encountered something nasty and unseen in the woods. In the final scene, we follow the shaky camera into a house. We hear a scream, recognize one of the characters standing silently in a dark corner with his back to us...and then the camera falls to the floor and the screen goes black.

THE BLAIR WITCH PROJECT, 1998

122 It comes to life!

Boris Karloff's first appearance as the aggrieved Egyptian mummy still has the power to send a shiver up anybody's spine. Sir Joseph Whemple: "'Death…eternal punishment…for…anyone…who…opens…this…casket. In the name…of Amon-Ra…the king of the gods.' Good heavens, what a terrible curse!" Assistant: "Well, let's see what's inside!"

THE MUMMY, 1932

123 Sooner or later they will find you

This is a great supernatural, haunted-house movie. While exploring the house, the children discover the graves of their servants, who are still working for them:
Anne: "Nicholas, don't speak to them!"
Nicholas: "Why?"
Anne: "They're dead!"

THE OTHERS, 2001

124 A mate... for the monster!

This film features many wonderful iconic horror images, but the best must be the bride's horrified, screaming face when she sees her husband-to-be for the first time.

THE BRIDE OF FRANKENSTEIN, 1935

125 "You don't know what Hugo's capable of..."

A guest at a ghostly Victorian mansion recounts his vision about a ventriloquist, Max, who is driven mad by his dummy, Hugo, which appears to come to life. In one scene, Max and Hugo are visited by another ventriloquist, who compliments Max on the act, but Hugo keeps butting in and then draws blood when he bites Max's hand.

DEAD OF NIGHT, 1945

126 "Do you know what the most frightening thing in the world is?"

A seemingly timid studio cameraman is filming a call girl. Suddenly, he produces a spike from one of the legs of his tripod and attaches a mirror to the front of his camera so his victim can watch herself die.

PEEPING TOM, 1960

127 Can they be stopped?

A group of youths explore an old house in the woods. They discover a demonic text and start to read it. Suddenly, the kids turn into demons—except for Ash, who has to contend with them all: "You bastards! Why are you doing this to me?"

THE EVIL DEAD, 1981

128 Don't waste your dying breath...

Evil scientist Raymond Lemorne dreams up a particularly nasty end for Rex, who wakes from a drugged sleep to discover he has been buried alive in a coffin. He uses his last lungful of air to scream for help.

THE VANISHING, 1988

129 Who will survive and what will be left of them?

Five innocent kids wander into the Texas badlands to investigate reports of grave robbing. A sliding door opens…and little Pammy falls into the mechanical teeth of Leatherface's chainsaw.

THE TEXAS CHAINSAW MASSACRE, 1974

130 Can you cheat death?

A plane full of high-school students is about to take off when one passenger has a terrifying premonition that the plane will crash. Desperate to get off, he causes such a riot that four other students and their teacher all get kicked out with him. Moments later, the plane explodes.

FINAL DESTINATION, 2000

131 Sweet dreams

A spooky and atmospheric tale of bloodsuckers terrorizing a small American town. In one scene, a young boy is terrified to see his dead brother floating outside and tapping on his bedroom window.

SALEM'S LOT, 1979

132 You'll wish it were only a nightmare...

The first appearance of the blade-wielding, hockey mask-wearing killer is an image that's likely to remain firmly embedded in anybody's mind.

FRIDAY THE 13TH, 1980

68

133 It takes a week

A mysterious videotape inflicts an agonizing death on anyone who watches it, seven days after the unwitting viewer sees the footage. Trust me, when you find out exactly what happens when the seven days are up…be prepared.

RING, 1998

134 Wake Up!

America's population is gradually being replaced by soulless alien replicas, born out of ghastly giant vegetable pods, who steal their bodies while they sleep. The frenzied McCarthy runs across a freeway screaming at the confused traffic, "You're next!"

INVASION OF THE BODY SNATCHERS, 1956

135 The great suspense film that shocked the world…and became a classic

A brutal man's wife and mistress lure him back to the mistress's lodgings, where his wife drugs him and his mistress drowns him in the bath. They dump the body in the swimming pool, only to find the next day that it has disappeared.

LES DIABOLIQUES, 1955

136 Now, he's writing to stay alive

Obsessed fan Annie Wilkes holds her favorite author, Paul Sheldon, prisoner in her home and prevents him from escaping by breaking both his legs with a sledgehammer. "I am your number-one fan. There is nothing to worry about. You are going to be just fine. I am your number one fan."

MISERY, 1990

137 Don't answer the phone. Don't open the door. Don't try to escape.

A beautiful teenager (Drew Barrymore) receives a threatening phone call from a stranger, who asks her about her favorite scary movies. Minutes later, her parents come home and find her body hanging from a tree in the garden.

SCREAM, 1996

138 At your own risk!

I love the scene in which humiliated Shakespearian thespian Vincent Price takes bloody revenge on a pompous theater critic by feeding him his own poodles.

THEATER OF BLOOD, 1973

139 Point taken

It's Halloween, and six-year-old Michael Myers's sister has been too busy amorously entertaining her boyfriend to notice that something is troubling her little brother—until he makes his point by stabbing her to death with a very large kitchen knife.

HALLOWEEN, 1978

140 "Sensible children... I have no power over them!"

This is the scariest Public Information Film ever inflicted on British schoolchildren. No youths went near a pond, lake, or quarry after seeing the faceless, hooded "spirit of dark and lonely water" drag children to their deaths in ponds full of old bikes and shopping carts.

LONELY WATER, 1973

141 Between Heaven and Hell, there's always Hollywood!

A writer realizes that the wallpaper in his Hollywood hotel is peeling. As he tries to press it back into place, paste starts to ooze between his fingers. It suddenly becomes clear that the entire place is one living, squelching, dripping mess.

BARTON FINK, 1991

142 She drove him bananas

The first scene, in which our great hairy friend King Kong holds the diminutive Jessica Lange in the palm of his hand, with his eyes filled with craving, is one of the most iconic images in cinema history.

KING KONG, 1976

143 Your mother was right

Young Jim Halsey is driving from Chicago to California to deliver a car. He is having trouble staying awake, so he decides to pick up a hitchhiker, remarking as he does so, "My mother told me to never do this." He's about to realize that Mom was right—the hitcher in his car, John Ryder, is actually a murderous psychopath.

THE HITCHER, 1986

144 A hard act to swallow!

We all require a bit of legal advice at some time in our lives, and perhaps it is because of this universal experience that one of the most popular scenes in this modern monster movie is when the lawyer is grabbed off the toilet and eaten by a huge Tyrannosaurus Rex.

JURASSIC PARK, 1993

145 Kill one and two take its place!

A horrific horde of crawl-and-crush giants claw their way out of the earth from mile-deep catacombs. "We may be witnessing a biblical prophecy come true—the beasts will reign over the earth."

THEM! 1954

146 Political palate

If you have ever wondered about the politics of vampires in eighteenth-century America, this scene is the perfect indicator.
Lestat: "Lord, what I wouldn't give for a drop of good old-fashioned Creole blood."
Louis: "Yankees are not to your taste?"
Lestat: "Their democratic flavor doesn't suit my palate, Louis."

INTERVIEW WITH THE VAMPIRE, 1994

147 When a murder case is this shocking, which do you trust... your emotions or the evidence?

Lawyer Teddy Barnes falls for her client, Jack Forrester, while defending him on a murder charge. He's bright, charming and—having inherited his wife's millions after someone took a knife to her—very rich. Is he guilty? The final scene will let you know!

JAGGED EDGE, 1985

148 What's a little murder among friends?

Three friends suddenly come into money when their new roommate dies mysteriously, leaving a suitcase full of cash. Juliet is chosen to hack the body of the deceased into easily disposable pieces. When she says she can't do it, Alex remarks, "But Juliet, you're a doctor. You kill people every day."

SHALLOW GRAVE, 1994

149 In space, no one can hear you scream.

Nostromo crewmember John Hurt seems to be fully recovered from his alien encounter, but at the crew's final feast, he is eating for two! His alien offspring suddenly performs its own gruesome cesarean at the dining table—it springs from his chest, smiles for the camera, and whizzes off to hide elsewhere on the gigantic spacecraft.

ALIEN, 1979

150 "Mother's not herself today..."

Thanks to Norman Bates, a secretary on the run, a minute of rapid cuts, a succession of shots of a figure entering the bathroom, and close-ups of a plunging knife, the shower curtain being pulled from its rod, and splattered blood, as well as the sound of shrieking violin strings—none of us will ever be comfortable in the shower again!

PSYCHO, 1960

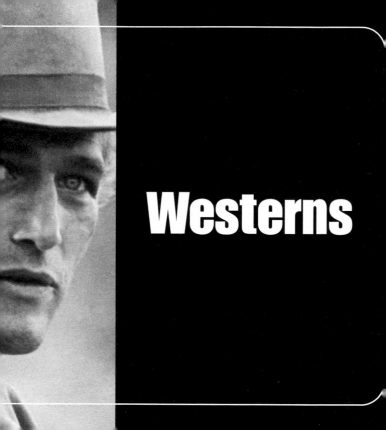

Westerns

Westerns are filmic tributes to the long-gone days of the wild American frontier and the remarkable pioneers who tried to tame it. These classic movies deal with the fundamentals—law and order, good and evil—and are usually teeming with massacres, saloon brawls, cattle herds, posses, cowboys, Indians, showdowns, and shootouts. The locations are spectacular and, in the hands of the right director, many Westerns have become masterpieces that continue to survive the test of time.

Previous page: Robert Redford and Paul Newman in
Butch Cassidy and the Sundance Kid (1969).

151 "If you can see them, they're not Apaches."

In a remote cavalry outpost, a disgruntled cavalry colonel (Henry Fonda) and a sensible, humanitarian captain (John Wayne) clash over a plan to lure the Apaches into their land and destroy them. The most unforgettable scene is the massacre—the gallop of the Indians' ponies and the tense drumming of the musical score become synchronized and work together to heighten the drama and tragedy of the inevitable slaughter.

FORT APACHE, 1948

152 "Do not forsake me, oh my darlin'."

A gang of riders wait for their recently pardoned leader at an isolated train station. They plan to get even with the town's sheriff as soon as their leader arrives. One of the men asks the stationmaster if the noon train is going to be on time. In a nervous little voice he answers, "Yes, sir!"

HIGH NOON, 1952

153 The picture that couldn't be stopped!

In a stable, Rio, played by Jane Russell (proud owner of a remarkable cleavage), wrestles in the hay. So provocative was this scene that the censors and the Catholic League of Decency came out against it.

THE OUTLAW, 1943

154 An army of one

The eponymous outlaw (Clint Eastwood) squares up to four uneasy soldiers who are after his blood: "Are you gonna draw those pistols or whistle Dixie?"

THE OUTLAW JOSEY WALES, 1976

155 For three men the civil war wasn't hell—it was practice!

There's going to be a showdown in a huge cemetery between three ruthless, gun-toting drifters—Blondie, "the Good", Senteza, "the Bad", and Tuco "the Ugly." The tension and action are intensified by Ennio Morricone's magnificent score.

THE GOOD, THE BAD AND THE UGLY, 1966

156 They'd never forget
the day he drifted into town

Clint Eastwood's enigmatic, nameless Stranger is never short of a disarming look or a snappy retort: "You're going to look pretty silly with that knife sticking out of your ass."
HIGH PLAINS DRIFTER, 1973

157 I don't run.
I don't hide. I go where I want. I do what I want.

History has painted a bloodthirsty picture of outlaw Billy the Kid, but in one scene of this film, the traditional image of the legendary gunslinger gives way to that of an innocent adolescent when the Kid enters into some boyish rough-and-tumble with his two companions.
THE LEFT-HANDED GUN, 1958

158 Now, a motion picture as big as all outdoors!

All the frontier spirit and prairie experience are in this musical, which is filled with such great lines as, "I wanted to marry her when I saw the moonlight shining on the barrel of her father's shotgun."
OKLAHOMA! 1955

159 Some say he's dead... some say he never will be.

A reclusive mountain trapper discovers a frozen body and a note: "I, Hatchet Jack, being of sound mind and broke legs, do leaveth my rifle to the next thing who finds it, Lord hope he be a white man. It is a good rifle, and killeth the bear that killeth me. Anyway, I am dead. Sincerely, Hatchet Jack."

JEREMIAH JOHNSON, 1972

160 He was one of the doggonedest, gawl-dingedest, dad-blamedest buckaroos that ever rode across these here United States of America!

After the film's prologue, which chronicles the heartless way in which the railroads stole away so many people's homes and farmlands as they ripped their way through the Midwest, the first train robbery seems almost heroic.

JESSE JAMES, 1939

161 A hero among men

A unit of the U.S. Cavalry, led by Major Dundee, chases murderous Apaches into Mexico to rescue three kidnapped white children. They succeed, but the expedition suddenly encounters a new threat—French troops—and only a suicidal sacrifice from an unexpected source will allow them to safely cross the border.

MAJOR DUNDEE, 1965

162 A man called "Horse" becomes an Indian warrior in the most electrifying ritual ever seen!

An English nobleman captured by Sioux Indians is forced to endure their rites of passage. In one, severed eagle's talons are thrust into the skin on the white man's chest, leather ropes are tied to the talons, and he is hoisted into the air, to be left to dangle painfully for hours above the ground.

A MAN CALLED HORSE, 1970

163 Every town has a story. Tombstone has a legend!

There is a confrontation in a saloon between Johnny Ringo and TB victim Doc Holliday. They test each other's knowledge of Latin, then Ringo tries some fancy gun twirling. The crowd applauds the smug villain, but Holliday wins the moment by producing his silver drinking cup, which he twirls like a pistol in a mocking manner.

TOMBSTONE, 1993

164 It all adds up to a classic Western

Three gunmen wait silently for a train; one drinks water from his hat, another tries to shoo away a fly. The train arrives, then leaves, as the haunting sound of a harmonica fills the air and a stranger suddenly appears. He asks where his horse is, but one of the gunmen snarls, "Looks like we're one horse short." "Looks like you brought two too many," Harmonica retorts.

ONCE UPON A TIME IN THE WEST, 1969

165 Sibling rivalry

Unaware that he is trespassing, Will Lockhart enters a small Mexican town, which is ruled by a blind and aging patriarch named Waggoman. Will is brutally beaten by the man's son, Dave, who wants to kill him, but Waggoman's adopted son, Vic, steps in just in time and saves Will's life.

THE MAN FROM LARAMIE, 1955

166 He's got to face a gunfight once more to live up to his legend

Aging gunfighter John Bernard Books (John Wayne), knowing that the cancer within him will soon end his days, winds up his affairs and heads to the saloon for one last gunfight. He wants to rid the town of the evil Mike Sweeney (Richard Boone), and to dissuade Gillom Rogers (Ron Howard), a young boy who idolizes him, from following in his footsteps.

THE SHOOTIST, 1976

167 In his own way, he is perhaps the most dangerous man who ever lived!

The poncho-wearing, cheroot-smoking "Man with No Name" subdues his anger when a gang of gunslingers pokes fun at his mule. He simply tells the coffin maker, "Get three coffins ready." Shortly after clearing up the problem, he adjusts his request: "My mistake, four coffins."

A FISTFUL OF DOLLARS, 1964

168 The epic journey of four generations of Americans who carved a country with their bare hands

Dedicated to the pioneers who opened up the Wild West, this movie explodes to life as the disgruntled Indians, provoked by the coming of the railroad, incite an enormous buffalo herd into a stampede.

HOW THE WEST WAS WON, 1962

169 A brand new brand of American frontier story

One-eyed marshal Rooster Cogburn confronts Ned Pepper and his gang across a wide expanse of open land. Rooster invites Pepper to surrender, but Pepper rudely declines: "Fill your hands, you son of a bitch." Rooster takes his reins between his teeth and charges at the outlaws in a chaotic blaze of rifle shots.

TRUE GRIT, 1969

170 They were seven—and they fought like seven hundred!

Three forlorn Mexican farmers hope to persuade gunfighter Chris Adams to take up their cause against bandits who are terrorizing their families. They offer him a small bundle of trinkets, which comprises everything of value in the village. Chris stares solemnly and says, "I have been offered a lot for my work, but never everything."

THE MAGNIFICENT SEVEN, 1960

171 It's that way-out whopper of a funny Western...A shebang to end all shebangs!

Who can forget the scene in this oddball cowboy musical when the drunken sot of a legendary gunslinger, Kid Shelleen, sobers up and gets spruced up in a fine new outfit?

CAT BALLOU, 1965

172 Outlawed! But fighting for an empire! Era of flaming feuds and new frontiers!

The theater curtain opens to reveal, standing on the stage, not the expected actress Lily Langtry, but horseman Cole Hardin, who is poised for a gunfight with Judge Bean. As Bean dies, he catches a fleeting glimpse of the woman of his dreams.

THE WESTERNER, 1940

173 You've seen nothing like 'em together...and in the heat and hate of Rio Bravo nothing can tear 'em apart!

In the blink of an eye, gun-toting sheriff John Wayne is clubbed, another man is knocked unconscious, and a third man is murdered.

RIO BRAVO, 1959

174 Nature in all its glory

The screen fills with an impressive line of dark clouds, then thunder and lightning, as the cavalry patrol passes through Monument Valley in this cinematic masterpiece.
SHE WORE A YELLOW RIBBON, 1949

175 John Ford's greatest romantic triumph

A conflict with the Apaches is imminent, and Lt. Col. Kirby Yorke (John Wayne) orders the women and children to be evacuated from his military post to safety. He selects his son, Jeff (Claude Jarman, Jr.), to escort them, saving Jeff from the deadly battle to come and rekindling the affections of his previously embittered ex-wife, Kathleen (Maureen O'Hara).
RIO GRANDE, 1950

176 A close shave

Wyatt Earp rides into Tombstone for a beer and a shave. He sits in the barber's chair and is lathered up, when gunshots suddenly shatter the silence—and the mirror. He asks, "What kind of a town is this, barber?"
MY DARLING CLEMENTINE, 1946

177

"There's a point where you either grow up and become a human being or you rot, like that bunch."

Link Jones appears to be every inch the good guy when he befriends his fellow train passengers, showgirl Billie Ellis and con man Sam Beasley. However, when the notorious Dock Tobin and his gang rob the train, the mild-mannered Link is revealed to be Tobin's nephew, and a former member of his gang of cutthroats.

THE MAN OF THE WEST, 1958

178 A real cliff-hanger

A charismatic duo is on the run from a posse that won't give up. They're trapped on a cliff's edge, with a neck-breaking drop to a river below them. One says to the other, "We can jump." The other responds that he can't swim. "What are you, crazy?" says the first. "The fall will probably kill you."

BUTCH CASSIDY AND THE SUNDANCE KID, 1969

179 Never give a saga an even break!

In Mel Brooks's mock Western, the townsfolk clear a path for the feared "man mountain," Mongo. From the safety of his saddle, another man scolds Mongo for illegally "parking" his animal. Mongo, with a single punch, knocks out the man's horse, and he shuffles into the saloon, ripping the doors off en route.

BLAZING SADDLES, 1974

180 "It's the first time the streamliner's stopped here in four years."

It's a warm day in 1945, and a train that doesn't usually stop in town, comes to a halt. Big-shouldered, one-armed stranger John J. Macreedy steps down from the train, under the intense scrutiny of the townsfolk. "Oh, I'll only be here 24 hours," he says. But the conductor warns him not to be so sure: "In a place like this, it could be a lifetime."

BAD DAY AT BLACK ROCK, 1955

181 They make the fighting, sinful West blaze into action before your eyes!

A sign reading "Welcome to Bottleneck" is struck by a bullet. More bullets smash whiskey bottles hanging from the sign. The camera pans slowly across Boot-Hill cemetery, shows a scene of utter mayhem—brawling, lawlessness, and gunplay—and ends with a view of the Last Chance Saloon.

DESTRY RIDES AGAIN, 1939

182 Lust in the dust!

In a hot border-town cantina, Pearl's Indian mother performs a sensual dance in front of her husband and her lover, to the whoops of a crowd of onlookers. She leaves with her lover, and young Pearl watches their silhouettes on a nearby building, horrified to see them being murdered.

DUEL IN THE SUN, 1946

183 Friends until the end

Two opposing soldiers face one another on a battlefield. One, Duke, is about to kill the other, who has already been seriously wounded, when he recognizes him as his old friend, Tod, from prewar days. But this is no lasting reunion—Duke is shot, and falls next to his dying friend. This is an explicitly racist landmark American film, and as President Woodrow Wilson once said, "It's like writing history with lightning. And my only regret is that it is all terribly true."

THE BIRTH OF A NATION, 1915

184 The mission that became a fortress, the fortress that became a shrine.

In the 13 days leading up to the battle of the Alamo, Davy Crockett has this to say: "Republic. I like the sound of the word. It means people can live free, talk free, go or come, buy or sell, be drunk or sober, however they choose. Some words give you a feeling. Republic is one of those words."

THE ALAMO, 1960

185 Big they fought! Big they loved! Big their story!

Retired sea captain James McKay is thought to be a coward because he doesn't believe in fistfights, but when ranch foreman Steve Leech insists on a brawl, McKay gives him a good lathering! We watch their marathon slugfest through a series of close-ups and long shots.

THE BIG COUNTRY, 1958

186 "Take 'em to Missouri, Matt!"

After breaking ranks with his embittered surrogate father and facing countless hardships to forge the Chisholm trail, cowboy Matt Garth successfully brings the herd into town, filling every street with cattle.

RED RIVER, 1948

187 All men are created equal

A slightly drunken Marmaduke Ruggles (Charles Laughton) masterfully recites Lincoln's Gettysburg Address to a saloon audience of cowhands and barflies.

RUGGLES OF RED GAP, 1935

188 "He'll be moving on one day, Joey. You'll be upset if you get to liking him too much."

In this memorable, echoing finale, Shane rides off into the bluish distance of the empty Wyoming landscape as Little Joey calls out, "Shane…Shane…Come back, Shane." But we know he never will.

SHANE, 1953

189 "If you'll take my advice, ma'am, you won't take this trip!"

The stage rounds a turn, a rifle shot is heard, and the camera tracks in to a close-up of the Ringo Kid. He stands tall in his boots, holding his saddle in one hand and twirling and recocking his Winchester rifle in the other: "Hold it!"

STAGECOACH, 1939

190 He's as stubborn as a mule

Cowboy Langland (Clark Gable) gets locked into a monumental one-on-one struggle with the feisty leader of a pack of wild horses to prove that he's the boss. He wins and recaptures the animal, then lets all the horses go free to satisfy his feisty new love, played by Marilyn Monroe.

THE MISFITS, 1961

191 Unchanged men in a changing land. Out of step, out of place and desperately out of time!

On the outskirts of a southwest Texas town, five men ride past a crowd of children, who are toying with scorpions they have placed in the middle of a colony of red fire ants. The giggling children watch as the struggling scorpions are tortured and consumed by the swarming ants.

THE WILD BUNCH, 1969

192 He had to find her... he had to find her...

John Wayne, as Ethan Edwards, tries to keep everyone's hopes up in the search for the little girl who has been kidnapped by Indians: "Our turnin' back don't mean nothin', not in the long run. She's alive, she's safe for a while. They'll keep her and raise her as one of their own. We'll find 'em. Just as sure as a turnin' of the earth."

THE SEARCHERS, 1956

193 **"There is an endless supply of white men, but there has always been a limited number of human beings."**

A historian is interviewing a wrinkled old man named Jack Crabb, who is quite energetic for his 121 years. Crabb starts to tell his story about the slaughter of Indian tribes by General Custer's troops by pointing at the tape recorder: "Turn that thing on and shut up! Now you just sit there and you'll learn something."

LITTLE BIG MAN, 1970

194 **"Did Pa used to kill folks?"**

Reformed gunfighter-turned-farmer William Munny digs out his old gun and, in a classic scene of out-of-practice target shooting, he misses the tin can with every shot. Blasting it with a shotgun instead, he tells his children, "If you have any problems, go see Sally Two Trees at Ned Logan's," then spurs on his horse and rides away.

UNFORGIVEN, 1992

195 "Hanging is any man's business that's around."

Gil Carter reads aloud the last letter of lynch-mob victim Donald Martin: "A man just naturally can't take the law into his own hands and hang people without hurtin' everybody in the world, 'cause then he's just not breaking one law, but all laws."

THE OX-BOW INCIDENT, 1943

196 The first Western!

Audiences gasped as a gun was fired straight at them from the big screen in this first ever Western, which was inspired by the Hole in the Wall gang's real-life robbery of the Union Pacific Railroad.

THE GREAT TRAIN ROBBERY, 1903

197 The man with the barbed-wire soul!

Hud confronts his father, who intends to shoot his entire herd of infected cattle to avoid an epidemic. The amoral Hud thinks his dad should sell the animals instead: "Why, this whole country is run on epidemics, where you been?" But his honest father won't listen, and the animals are slaughtered, in a harrowing scene.

HUD, 1963

198 It's God's land

Young cowhand Billy Grimes makes a stand to support a group of religious pilgrims facing the wrath of an irate land baron. He sets a precedent for the other cowboys, who feel compelled to take up arms and join him.

THE CULPEPPER CATTLE CO. 1972

199 The Civil War had ended, but one man's battle with himself was just beginning...

Lieutenant John Dunbar is alone at his deserted frontier post, with only a wild wolf and the nearby Sioux nation for company: "If it wasn't for my companion, I believe I'd be having the time of my life."

DANCES WITH WOLVES, 1990

200 Sometimes you've got to lay your cards on the table

While playing cards, the Virginian is insulted by another player: "When I want to know anything from you, I'll tell you, you long-legged son of a bitch." The eponymous hero coolly lays his gun on the table and responds, "If you want to call me that, smile!"

THE VIRGINIAN, 1929

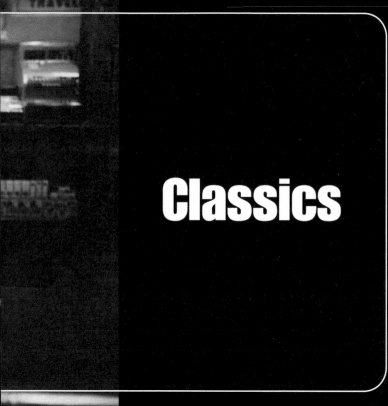

Classics

Some movies are universally acknowledged as being truly remarkable pieces of cinema. They possess unique, sometimes indefinable qualities that have enabled them to stand the test of time and capture the hearts of viewers for decades. This chapter celebrates these traditional masterpieces of the cinema. But it also recognizes a few wonderful movies that may have been overlooked in the past, as well as several more recent films that will no doubt be perceived as classics in the future. Countless movie moments merit a place here, but only a few could be chosen.

Previous page: Marilyn Monroe and Don Murray in *Bus Stop* (1956).

201 That immortal line...

Rhett Butler's (Clark Gable) exasperated parting from his wife Scarlett (Vivien Leigh) at their front door is an unforgettable scene. She begs him, "Rhett, if you go, where shall I go? What shall I do?" and he coolly responds, without any sign of sentiment, "Frankly, my dear, I don't give a damn!"

GONE WITH THE WIND, 1939

202 Not every gift is a blessing

Cole Sear (Haley Joel Osment) uses his ability to talk to spirits to mentally demolish his teacher by reminding him of his past stuttering problem and his childhood nickname, "Stuttering Stanley."

THE SIXTH SENSE, 1999

203 A man of many parts

No matter which is your favorite moment from this all-time classic, the line that will stick in your mind comes wrapped in a thick fake German accent, when Dr. Strangelove (Peter Sellers) gets up from his wheelchair and ecstatically announces, "Mein Führer, I can walk!"

DR. STRANGELOVE, OR: HOW I LEARNED TO STOP WORRYING AND LOVE THE BOMB, 1964

204 What if...

In this movie's most famous scene, Terry is in a taxi with his brother Charley, who is desperately trying to stop him from testifying against the local labor bosses. When bribery and threats fail, Charley pulls a gun on his brother. Terry launches into a speech full of sadness, regret, and accusation: "I coulda had class. I coulda been a contender. I coulda been somebody, instead of a bum, which is what I am, let's face it."

ON THE WATERFRONT, 1954

205 Hearts of darkness

Lieutenant Colonel Kilgore orders a massive helicopter attack on an unsuspecting, and seemingly innocent, Vietnamese village. The helicopters glide through the breaking light like a flock of birds, following Kilgore's orders: "We'll come in low out of the rising sun, and about a mile out, we'll put on the music...Yeah, use Wagner. Scares the hell out of the slopes. My boys love it."

APOCALYPSE NOW, 1979

206 This time it's war

Ripley climbs inside a robotic power loader and comes through the cargo bay door to rescue young Newt from the alien queen, yelling, "Get away from her, you bitch!" What follows is one of the greatest fight scenes ever filmed, as Ripley and the alien, led by their maternal instincts, battle to destroy one another.

ALIENS, 1986

207 "I am torn by desire…tortured by hate!"

In the final scene, the ghosts of Cathy and Heathcliff are reunited at their imaginary castle on Peniston Crag on the Yorkshire moors, where they had earlier declared their eternal love.

WUTHERING HEIGHTS, 1939

208 "I think she's got it, I think she's got it."

Professor Higgins's pupil, Cockney flower girl Eliza Doolittle, suddenly masters the vocal exercises he's been bombarding her with and all traces of her coarse accent simply disappear, causing Higgins to gleefully exclaim, "By George, she's got it!"

MY FAIR LADY, 1964

209 Make a note of this

After enjoying Mozart's new opera, Emperor Joseph II pays tribute to the composer, but remarks that the opera had too many notes—and that Mozart should get rid of a few here and there!

AMADEUS, 1984

210 Hunted by men…Sought by women!

In the bleak closing scene, Holly waits on the tree-lined cemetery road for Anna. Anna walks down the long, empty road straight past him, without even glancing at Holly, the man who betrayed her lover. Holly lights a cigarette, and the screen fades to black.

THE THIRD MAN, 1949

211 The smell of greasepaint

Third-rate entertainer Archie Rice (Laurence Olivier) warns his audience not to try leaving, because they have been locked in. He then launches into his painfully authentic music-hall act. He gives a fine soft-shoe shuffle as he starts to sing, "If they see that you're blue, they'll walk out on you…"

THE ENTERTAINER, 1960

212 In a war without heroes they are kings

In a rather poignant scene, Troy Barlow and his Iraqi interrogator both talk about their newborn children and how war has affected their lives. Despite their cultural differences, the confrontation brings them to a closer understanding of each other.

THREE KINGS, 1999

213 Trains that pass in the night

Ill-fated lovers Laura and Alec have come to the end of their clandestine weekly meetings, but before they can say their final goodbyes at the railway station, they are interrupted by an acquaintance. Alec gently places his hand on Laura's shoulder, then disappears forever.

BRIEF ENCOUNTER, 1945

214 Two men chasing dreams of glory!

The iconic image from this movie is of the Olympic athletes running, in slow motion, along the beach in the surf. The scene is brilliantly underscored by Vangelis's instantly recognizable score.

CHARIOTS OF FIRE, 1981

215 Like it or not

While Osgood Fielding III drives Joe (dressed as Josephine) and Jerry (dressed as Daphne) out to his yacht, Jerry tries to explain why he cannot marry him—he smokes, he can never have children, and so on. In final desperation, Jerry pulls off his wig and reveals that he is a man. The unshakable millionaire simply shrugs and says, "Well, nobody's perfect."

SOME LIKE IT HOT, 1959

216 "Well, there's something you don't see every day."

The demon Gozer lets the Ghostbusters imagine their own means of destruction. Peter urges them to clear their minds, but Ray tries to think of something harmless from his childhood that could never hurt them. Then the ground starts to shake, and the boys catch sight of a giant Stay Puft Marshmallow Man between New York's skyscrapers. The huge marshmallow sailor, with his permanent grin, has come to do battle.

GHOSTBUSTERS, 1984

217 Wonderful! Wonderful! Wonderful!

At the end of Frank Capra's Christmas classic, humble, hardworking George Bailey finds out just how much his selflessness has meant to his family, friends, and community, and he realizes that he is "the richest man in town."

IT'S A WONDERFUL LIFE, 1946

218 Can't see the forest for the trees

Three aspiring New York models plot to marry millionaires. One of them agrees to spend a weekend with a man at his "lodge," believing that the "lodge" is a fraternity he belongs to. However, she arrives to find herself at a little cabin in the wilderness, where she gets snowed in and has to be rescued by a penniless forest ranger.

HOW TO MARRY A MILLIONAIRE, 1953

219 "I can't help it."

This movie includes a captivating image of leggy temptress Lola Frohlich (Marlene Dietrich) wearing a tilted top hat and singing "Falling in Love Again" in a sleazy German nightclub.

THE BLUE ANGEL, 1930

220 The classic story of power and the press

The camera focuses on a snow-covered house, then pulls back to reveal that the house is inside a snow globe, which is resting in the palm of a man's hand. The word "rosebud" is whispered, and the globe falls to the floor, rolls, and shatters. The mystery has begun.

CITIZEN KANE, 1941

221 "It could be the most terrifying motion picture I have ever made!"

Melanie sits on a school swing, smoking a cigarette, unaware of the hundreds of crows silently gathering behind her. As the sound of children singing wafts from the school, Melanie catches sight of one bird in midair, and she watches as it lands on the packed jungle gym.

THE BIRDS, 1963

222 What drove her to do it?

Elegant widow Daisy Werthan is inching her car out of the garage when her foot slips. She suddenly guns the engine and reverses across the flowerbeds and over a wall. She tries to explain to her son that the "car misbehaved" but he knows better. "Cars don't misbehave, Mama," he says. "They have to be caused to misbehave."

DRIVING MISS DAISY, 1989

223 Star tantrum

The opening scene is of a cartoon called "Somethin's Cookin'," starring Baby Herman and his babysitter, Roger Rabbit. The baby keeps putting himself in danger while trying to get a cookie, but Roger saves him every time—by getting hurt himself. The cartoon ends with a refrigerator landing on the poor rabbit, who sees tweeting bluebirds circling his head. Suddenly a director shouts, "Cut!" and Baby Herman storms off the set, gnawing a cigar—he is angry at Roger for changing the script and seeing birds instead of stars.

WHO FRAMED ROGER RABBIT, 1988

224 Harrowing

This heartfelt telling of the tragedy of the unsinkable ship *Titanic* portrays the unquestionable acts of selflessness of real people. One father musters all his confidence and love to usher his wife and three children into a lifeboat, knowing that he is condemned to go down with the ship and that this is his very last moment with those he loves. As the small craft is lowered and their faces drop from his gaze, his brave face slips to reveal his true despair.

A NIGHT TO REMEMBER, 1958

225 All things being equal...

Abraham Lincoln, in his stovepipe hat, insists on continuing his walk despite a gathering rainstorm: "No, I think I might go on a piece. Maybe to the top of that hill." The film ends with a shot of his statue at the Lincoln Memorial.

YOUNG MR. LINCOLN, 1939

226 The Daddy of them all

The image of sexually frustrated Maggie (Elizabeth Taylor) in a slinky camisole remains fixed in mind, but the greatest moment of this film may be the confrontation in the cellar between her husband Brick (Paul Newman) and Big Daddy (Burl Ives).

CAT ON A HOT TIN ROOF, 1958

227 One for the road

Full of liquor and remorse, Burt Lancaster pours his heart out to Montgomery Clift, who is being unfairly treated for refusing to box. They sit in the middle of the road, sharing a bottle, both ready to be killed by the next vehicle that comes along, yet also wishing to save one another from their plights. They are brothers-in-arms—each ready to lay down his life for the other.

FROM HERE TO ETERNITY, 1953

228

"Boycott Sal's famous pizzeria!"

As the heat in New York rises, the tension and tempers in the neighborhood rise to match it. An African-American named Buggin Out asks Sal, the owner of the local pizzeria, why the photos on his Wall of Fame are all of famous white Italians when the restaurant is in a predominantly black area. Buggin Out insists that Sal "put some brothers" on the wall, but Sal refuses, and the tension continues to rise.

DO THE RIGHT THING, 1989

229 The coming of age of Bo Decker… and the girl who made him a man!

After pulling over at a rest stop during a snowstorm, bus driver Carl (Robert Bray) can no longer stand the way testosterone-driven cowboy Bo Decker (Don Murray) is treating pretty showgirl Cherie (Marilyn Monroe). He sets about teaching him how to treat a lady—in a fistfight to remember.

BUS STOP, 1956

230 Stranger in a strange land

Tess Harding's (Katharine Hepburn) attempts to be a domesticated housewife end in disaster as she wrestles with several kitchen appliances and ruins the breakfast as Sam Craig (Spencer Tracy) watches in disbelief.

WOMAN OF THE YEAR, 1942

231 "Go where the wind blows."

At dinner in his hotel, Gustav von Aschenbach (Dirk Bogarde) asks the concierge how long the sirocco wind will last, and he is given the most convoluted reply imaginable. The concierge then slinks away, rolling his eyes and hoping that he has gotten away with his answer.

DEATH IN VENICE, 1971

232 Fogbound

Several rich and famous people have their lives thrown into turmoil by an unexpected delay at a London airport. Movie mogul Max Buda greets his financial wizard, Dr. Schwatzbacher, with a kiss on the lips, and the two discuss a plan to avoid paying tax on Buda's next film by shooting it in the Friendly Isles.

THE V.I.P.S, 1963

233 A Hollywood story

Norma Desmond elegantly descends her marble staircase, imagining that she is playing the most important scene of her career. At the bottom of the stairs, she pauses and speaks to the crew, promising never to leave them again, and then slips back into character saying, "All right, Mr. DeMille, I'm ready for my close-up."

SUNSET BOULEVARD, 1950

234 There but for the grace of God

As the Joad family travel in their dilapidated old truck along Highway 66, the camera looks through the windscreen at their faces as they gaze out at the desert beyond, and it travels with them as they arrive in the impoverished shantytown, Hooverville.

THE GRAPES OF WRATH, 1940

235 Sore loser

Drunk and losing at poker, Stanley goes mad and starts attacking his wife, Stella. Pandemonium breaks out as his friends try to restrain him and hold him under a cold shower to sober him up. When he realizes what he has done, Stanley searches for his wife. He stands in the street in a torn, wet T-shirt calling, "Stellaaaah!"

A STREETCAR NAMED DESIRE, 1951

236 Loves and fishes

Living at their grandparents' house during World War II, Bill and Sue Rowan are sent out fishing. The children try and try, mindful of their grandfather's warning not to come home empty-handed, but they fail to catch any fish. Just as they are about to give up, a sudden bomb blast stuns all the fish in the river. The fish come floating up to the surface, where they can be easily collected.

HOPE AND GLORY, 1987

237 Home sweet home

The Wizard of Oz's hot-air balloon accidentally slips from its tether and drifts away, leaving Dorothy and Toto stranded in Oz—but not forever. Dorothy learns that her ruby slippers will carry her back to Kansas, so she closes her eyes, clicks her heels together, and says, "There's no place like home."

THE WIZARD OF OZ, 1939

238 All your Christmases rolled into one

After being taught the meaning of Christmas by three spirits, Ebenezer Scrooge procures the biggest turkey in the neighborhood and sets off to join the Cratchit family in their Christmas festivities, causing Tiny Tim to utter his immortal line, "God bless us everyone."

A CHRISTMAS CAROL, 1984

239 A room with a view

We watch a beautiful young woman, bathed in warm lamplight, through her window as she massages her hands, arms, shoulders, and breasts with lemons. The camera pulls back, and we realize that she is also being watched by an old man from across the street.

ATLANTIC CITY, 1980

240 Never one to mince his words

George C. Scott's epic portrayal of the arrogant yet colorful World War II general begins with a classic monologue in front of a giant American flag: "Now I want you to remember that no bastard ever won a war by dying for his country. He won it by making the other poor dumb bastard die for his country."

PATTON, 1970

241 Mexican wave

Fred C. Dobbs (Humphrey Bogart) is up against some Mexican bandits, who try to bluff him. He asks them to show him some identification, and he gets an unforgettable reply: "Badges? We ain't got no badges. We don't need no badges. I don't have to show you any stinking badges."

THE TREASURE OF THE SIERRA MADRE, 1948

242 You must remember this

A beautiful woman walks into Rick's Bar in Casablanca and immediately recognizes the piano player, Sam. She urges him to play some of the old songs: "Play it once, Sam, for old times' sake." Sam bluffs that he cannot remember the song she requests, so she hums the first few bars. Kind-natured Sam gives in and begins his classic rendition of "As Time Goes By." Rick hears him and angrily storms over to the piano, saying, "Sam, I thought I told you never to play..." And then he sees her...

CASABLANCA, 1942

243 "It's Brigadoon!"

Gareth attends Carrie's Scottish wedding, suitably dressed for the occasion in a kilt and stockings. He makes a grand entrance into the ballroom with an American woman on his arm, who asks him if he knows Oscar Wilde. He replies, "not personally, but I know someone who could get you his fax number."

FOUR WEDDINGS AND A FUNERAL, 1994

244 Boy, girl, boy, girl...

A beautiful friendship begins when showbiz stars Phil Davis and Bob Wallace go to see the Haynes Sisters' act as a favor to their old army pal, "freckle-faced Haynes." They discover that the girls are in trouble with the local sheriff, who is at the nightclub to arrest them. Bob and Phil send the girls on ahead to the railroad station, then stall the police by doing their act for them. They don minimalist drag outfits and go onstage to perform a song called "Sisters."

WHITE CHRISTMAS, 1954

245 A rebel with a cause

Barry Fitzgerald plays Michaleen Flynn, the local majordomo, bookmaker, matchmaker, and much more. He wanders toward the pub one wet and windy night, memorably muttering, "It's a fine, soft night, so I think I'll go join me comrades and talk a little treason."

THE QUIET MAN, 1952

246 The greatest adventure a man ever lived…with a woman!

Charlie Allnut (Humphrey Bogart) and Rose Sayer (Katharine Hepburn) set off in their faithful little steamboat to sink a German warship. Rose has a plan to get revenge for the death of her brother, and she asks Charlie, "Could you make a torpedo?"

THE AFRICAN QUEEN, 1951

247 Don't shoot the messenger

After Marian Maudsley takes him into town and buys him a striking green outfit, the innocent youth Leo falls for the beautiful young woman, but she just wants Leo to be her delivery boy. She asks him to take messages to farmer Ted Burgess, and she warns him to keep them a secret from Viscount Trimingham, her fiancé.

THE GO-BETWEEN, 1970

248 "Would you like me to seduce you?"

The seduction of Dustin Hoffman's Benjamin Braddock by Anne Bancroft's Mrs. Robinson, is a classic scene. After Benjamin stutters, "Mrs. Robinson, you're trying to seduce me," she gives a saucy chuckle, and the camera frames her young victim on the screen with her stockinged leg.

THE GRADUATE, 1967

249 He was a winner... He was a loser... He was a hustler.

Jackie Gleason is excellent as poolroom pro Minnesota Fats. He is as cool as a cucumber in the first tournament when he takes on the talented young hustler Eddie Felson (Paul Newman), who has been waiting a long time to play him.

THE HUSTLER, 1961

250 Touché

Indiana Jones comes face to face with an impressive Arab swordsman who is waving his sword around threateningly. We half expect a duel until Indy, looking bored, just gets out his pistol and shoots him.

RAIDERS OF THE LOST ARK, 1981

Science Fiction

Science Fiction movies are visionary and imaginative contributions to our cinematic diet. Sometimes founded on the seeds of a past or future reality, they inevitably involve futuristic technology, fantastic settings, heroes, villains, and incredible special effects. These movies regularly focus on space or time travel, people or animals exposed to dangerous chemicals, encounters with aliens, fantastic journeys, or end-of-the-world scenarios. Sci-fi films often conceal deeper meanings that express man's anxieties about technology and the future, or feature epic battles between the forces of good and evil. Armed only with a bucket of popcorn, any one of us can enter the cinema and become the survivor of an alien attack or apocalyptic event.

Previous page: Peter Sellers in *Dr. Strangelove, or: How I Learned to Stop Worrying and Love the Bomb* (1964).

251 May the force be with you

The old hermit Ben Kenobi removes something from a chest and gives it to Luke Skywalker. It's a light saber, the weapon of choice of a Jedi knight, which has been passed down from Luke's father. He tells Luke, "A young Jedi named Darth Vader, who was a pupil of mine until he turned to evil…betrayed and murdered your father. Vader was seduced by the Dark Side of the Force."

STAR WARS, 1977

252 Man has made his match… Now it's his problem

In the 21st century, in an apocalyptic world of hover cars and robotics, Blade Runner Deckard (Harrison Ford) gets his wish— the death of replicant Roy Batty (Rutger Hauer), who provides an unexpected final soliloquy: "I've seen things you people wouldn't believe. Attack ships on fire off the shoulder of Orion. I watched c-beams glitter in the dark near Tanhauser Gate. All those moments will be lost in time like tears in rain. Time to die…" Batty expires in the rain, and a white dove flies upward…

BLADE RUNNER, 1982

253 The story that touched the world!

Elliot and his brother take E.T. out "trick-or-treating" with them on Halloween night. E.T. is dressed up as a ghost, pretending to be Elliot's little sister, Gertie. Their mom thinks they look cute, so she takes a photograph of them—and the brilliance of the flash makes E.T. faint.

E.T. THE EXTRA-TERRESTRIAL, 1982

254 Earth's darkest day will be man's finest hour

A. J. (Ben Affleck) is on the launchpad, about to board a space shuttle, when he starts to sing "I'm Leaving on a Jet Plane" to his fiancée, Grace (Liv Tyler). All the other roughnecks join in as he sweeps her up into his arms in a classic Hollywood embrace.

ARMAGEDDON, 1998

255 250 years in the future, all will be lost unless the fifth element is found

The breathtaking and rather Utopian view of a futuristic New York cityscape filled with hundreds of flying cars is so well done that not only is it mesmerizing, it also makes it easy to imagine that one day the world may be like that.

THE FIFTH ELEMENT, 1997

256 Flying saucers invade our planet!

This movie uses wonderful special effects to show aliens invading Earth. We watch as Washington, D.C. is obliterated by cone-headed aliens in classically designed flying saucers. The military's position is clear: "When an armed and threatening power lands uninvited in our capital, we don't meet him with tea and cookies!"

EARTH VS. THE FLYING SAUCERS, 1956

257 H. G. Wells's astounding adventure!

Helped immeasurably by fantastic special effects, an eccentric professor (Lionel Jeffries) and his friends blast off to the moon in their rather primitive spaceship. How did they achieve it? By applying a liberal amount of antigravity paint to their spherical metallic spacecraft, of course!

FIRST MEN IN THE MOON, 1964

258 Steve Martin plays a world-famous surgeon. He invented screw-top, zip-lock brain surgery. Trust him.

In one harebrained scene, brain surgeon Dr. Michael Hfuhruhurr (Steve Martin) must complete a drunk-driving test to the satisfaction of the Austrian police.

THE MAN WITH TWO BRAINS, 1983

259 "Klaatu barada nikto." From out of space... a warning and an ultimatum!

In the film's unforgettable final scene, the soft-spoken extra-terrestrial Klaatu makes a disarmament speech to scientists and world leaders, "...but if you threaten to extend your violence, this Earth of yours will be reduced to a burned-out cinder. Your choice is simple. Join us and live in peace, or pursue your present course and face obliteration. We shall be waiting for your answer. The decision rests with you."

THE DAY THE EARTH STOOD STILL, 1951

260 Hotline suspense comedy

The president of the United States (Peter Sellers) makes a telephone call to his Russian counterpart to relay some difficult news: "Now then, Dmitri, you know how we've always talked about the possibility of something going wrong with the bomb. The *bomb*, Dmitri. The *hydrogen* bomb! Well now, what happened is, uh, one of our base commanders, he had a sort of, well, he went a little funny in the head. You know. Just a little...funny. And, uh, he went and did a silly thing..."

DR. STRANGELOVE, OR: HOW I LEARNED TO STOP WORRYING AND LOVE THE BOMB, 1964

261 It's only a state of mind

At a time when bureaucracy and government control has run amok, one cog in the wheel, Sam Lowry, spots a paperwork mistake that led to the arrest of an innocent man—then he makes the mistake of trying to put it right.

Sam Lowry: "I only know you got the wrong man."

Jack Lint: "Information Transit got the wrong man. I got the right man. The wrong one was delivered to me as the right man, I accepted him on good faith as the right man. Was I wrong?"

BRAZIL, 1985

262 He was never in time for his classes... He wasn't in time for his dinner...Then one day...he wasn't in his time at all.

Marty McFly hasn't only broken the time barrier, he's also ruined his parents' first date! He's created an anomaly in time that threatens his own existence...he begins to fade away until his dad-to-be finally manages to excuse himself and kisses the girl he'll later marry. Phew!

BACK TO THE FUTURE, 1985

263 It came from outer space

Young Hogarth Hughes befriends a giant robot who falls to Earth and eats his television antenna. Trying to bridge the gap between their understanding of each other, they tackle the difficult subject of death. The child explains that everything dies, but that everything also has a soul—even the robot—and that souls go on forever. When he leaves, the robot looks up at the stars and says, "Souls don't die."

THE IRON GIANT, 1999

264 We've always believed we weren't alone

After a tremendous dogfight through the Arizona desert in which his fighter plane is destroyed, Will Smith pulls open the alien spacecraft that has crash-landed nearby and punches the alien straight in the face. "Welcome to Earth!"

INDEPENDENCE DAY, 1996

265 A futuristic comic feast

An unemployed clown arrives at a butcher shop beneath an ancient tenement building, looking for work. Meat, like all food at this futuristic time, is in short supply, and unbeknownst to him, the butcher is also the landlord, who looks after his tenants with occasional offcuts of fattened-up handymen.

DELICATESSEN, 1991

266 Alex Gardner has an extraordinary gift. To keep it may cost him his life…

Psychic Alex Gardner has the ability to telepathically enter other people's dreams, so he helps Doctor Paul Novotny with his project to eliminate nightmare-related insomnia. In one memorable sequence, we enter a child's nightmare that involves a creepy Lizard Man.

DREAMSCAPE, 1984

267 An evil robot is brought to life

Fritz Lang's vision of the 21st century has one particularly memorable scene. Mad scientist Rotwang hooks Maria up to his laboratory paraphernalia to use her circulatory system and likeness to bring an evil robot duplicate to life via a series of glowing hula-hoops passed over her body.

METROPOLIS, 1927

268 It'll end in tears…

In this sci-fi classic, a team of specialists is miniaturized and sent on a mission aboard a minuscule submarine to cure an ill, but indispensable, scientist from the inside—a terrific scene itself! But it's when Raquel Welch gets attacked by gooey white antibodies that things *really* get interesting.

FANTASTIC VOYAGE, 1966

269 In the future, there will be no war. There will only be Rollerball.

In a futuristic society, corporations use the violent sport Rollerball to control and subdue the people because it demonstrates the futility of resistance and individuality. When superstar player Jonathan E. becomes too popular and powerful, the corporations use threats to get him to retire. But he defies them and fights for his freedom, and, as his team enters the arena, a huge, hyped-up crowd chants "JON-A-THAN! JON-A-THAN! JON-A-THAN! JON-A-THAN!"

ROLLERBALL, 1975

270 An alien encounter!

After umpteen hours of thrill-infested danger, Ripley sets the fuses for the spacecraft *Nostromo* to be blown to smithereens. With claxons sounding and steam venting everywhere, she grabs Jones, the ship's cat, and runs for the safety of the escape vessel. Once aboard, she fires the thrusters and takes off just as the mother ship explodes. Is it safe? Is it hell!

ALIEN, 1979

271 Do you remember...the future?

Marty McFly runs out of the Café '80s toward two little girls on what look like scooters. He grabs hold of one of them and says, "Hey! Hey, little girl, I need to borrow your...Hoverboard?" He throws the futuristic wheel-less skateboard down, and it hovers above the ground. He jumps on and swiftly masters it.

BACK TO THE FUTURE PART II, 1989

272 The adventure continues...

Who could possibly forget the startling revelation that comes out during the amazing light-saber showdown between Luke Skywalker and Darth Vader? Vader cuts off Luke's hand with one swift movement and, as Luke backs away, Vader coldly says, "Luke, I am your father."

THE EMPIRE STRIKES BACK, 1980

273 The rules are simple: once you go in, you don't come out!

The scene you'll remember from this film is when Snake Plissken (Kurt Russell) makes his fantastic silent-glider approach into Manhattan, which has become a high-security prison!

ESCAPE FROM NEW YORK, 1981

274 Eat your greens...

In 2022, the world is bleak and overpopulated, and food is rare. The authorities have managed to relieve the food shortage with an unknown manufactured food called Soylent Green. In one poignant episode, Sol Roth lies on a slab watching scenes of nature and beauty projected around him as he dies...then Detective Robert Thorn discovers the truth about Soylent Green.

SOYLENT GREEN, 1973

275 He said "I'll be back" and he meant it!

Young John Connor, destined leader of the human resistance, teaches his robot protector a few phrases to help him blend in. John Connor: "No, no, no, no. You gotta listen to the way people talk. You don't say 'affirmative,' or some shit like that. You say 'no problemo.' And if someone comes on to you with an attitude, you say 'eat me.' And if you want to shine them on, it's 'hasta la vista, baby.'"
The Terminator: "Hasta la vista, baby."

TERMINATOR 2: JUDGMENT DAY, 1991

276 The future will not be user-friendly

Neo (Keanu Reeves) goes to see the Oracle, who will be able to tell him if he is "The One." She tells him not to worry about the vase. He turns around to look for a vase, and accidentally knocks one over, smashing it. "Oh," says the Oracle, "what's really going to bake your noodle later on is, would you still have broken it if I hadn't said anything?"

THE MATRIX, 1999

277 Mighty panorama of Earth-shaking fury as an army from Mars invades!

As aliens once again attack our vulnerable little planet, the collective minds of the military and science come together to work out a strategy to defeat them:
Major General Mann: "Pattern-wise, one lands, then two, making groups of threes joined magnetically. Is that possible?"
Dr. Clayton Forrester: "If they do it, it is."

THE WAR OF THE WORLDS, 1953

278 Somewhere in the universe, there must be something better than man!

It's one thing for an astronaut to crash-land on an alien planet, and quite another to be constantly chased and persecuted by the ruling apes. And just when you thought there might be some hope of returning to Earth and everything you cherish, you stumble upon a statue on the beach that looks all too familiar…

PLANET OF THE APES, 1968

279 Old West meets the microchip

Two city guys vacation in Westworld, a fantasy resort where people interact with humanlike robots. The guys get outfitted in full cowboy gear, including guns and holsters, and mosey off to the saloon, where a gunslinger in black provokes them. One of the two urban cowboys tells the other to "kill him," so they square up for a gunfight. The man in black is too slow on the draw, and he falls to the floor, "dead." Of course, he is only a robot, and he can be repaired…

WESTWORLD 1973

280 Amazing!

Despite being one of only two survivors of a hideous monster roaming their planet, Altaira Morbius (Anne Francis) is still determined to look her best. She owns several stunning outfits, but she instructs Robby the Robot to make her a new dress when Commander John Adams (Leslie Nielsen) comes to investigate.

Altaira: "But it must be different—absolutely nothing must show—below, above or through."

Robot: "Radiation-proof?"

Altaira: "No, just eye-proof."

FORBIDDEN PLANET, 1956

281 Return to a galaxy...far, far away

Our heroes reach the shield generator on Endor. After a helpful Ewok distracts three Imperial Storm Troopers by stealing their speeder bikes, Han Solo sneaks up behind a fourth. He uses an old trick to gain the upper hand—tapping the Storm Trooper on his right shoulder and then appearing on his left. The Trooper falls for it and is led into a trap.

RETURN OF THE JEDI, 1983

282 "I'm sorry Dave..."

Computer HAL 9000 has become unreliable. Worse—irrational. Captains Dave Bowman and Frank Poole withdraw to the safety of a soundproof pod on the spacecraft *Discovery* and conspire to shut HAL down. What they don't realize is that this computer can lip-read!

2001: A SPACE ODYSSEY, 1968

283 The future is history

Bruce Willis is sent back through time to retrieve a sample of a deadly virus in an effort to stop millions of people dying from a plague in 2035. The attempts to get him to the right time period are hit-and-miss and he ends up in a lunatic asylum in 1990 trying to convince the doctors of his mission—and his sanity: "Oh, wouldn't it be great if I was crazy? Then the world would be OK."

12 MONKEYS, 1995

284 Not fans of country music

Sci-fi movies have a knack for placing the solution to our problems right under our noses. In the case of mega-spoof *Mars Attacks!* it becomes clear that the terrifying little bug-eyed visitors from outer space have a tendency to explode when they hear Grandma's gramophone playing Slim Whitman yodeling!

MARS ATTACKS! 1996

285 Bombed out in space with a spaced-out bomb!

On a mission to destroy unstable suns that threaten Earth, hippie astronauts fight boredom, aliens, and a malfunctioning computer. In one episode, a crew member tries to convince Bomb 20 not to blow up the spaceship by tricking it with logic, philosophy, and theology...

DARK STAR, 1974

286 Just because they're old, it doesn't mean they're dead!

After construction workers discover a skull in London, a full archaeological dig uncovers more skulls and a cylindrical shell that looks like an unexploded bomb. The shell is pried open and what appear to be dead insectlike creatures are found inside.

QUATERMASS AND THE PIT, 1967

287 One in the eye for science

The special effects in this first sci-fi movie, made by imaginative French filmmaker Georges Méliès, thrilled early audiences. Through pioneering techniques, trick photography, and superimposed images, audiences were able to watch a rocket ship blast off into space from a launching cannon and crash-land in the eye of the man in the moon!

A TRIP TO THE MOON, 1902

288 What would you do if you were accused of a murder you had not committed...yet?

To prevent murders in 2054, the Pre-Crime Division of the police force uses the precognitive powers of three genetically altered humans. In one crucial scene, Detective John Anderton (Tom Cruise) picks up the small red ball that arrives in the "perpetrator chute" and realizes that his own name is engraved on it. The precogs have predicted that he will kill a man he doesn't even know in less than 36 hours!

MINORITY REPORT, 2002

289 Instead of putting out fires, firemen now burn books...

In one scene, Guy Montag reads a forbidden book he's smuggled home. It is Dickens's David Copperfield. As he reads the words aloud, the camera moves in closer, until the entire screen is filled with the words he's reading.

Guy: "Do you remember what you asked me the other day; if I ever read the books I burn? Remember?"

Clarisse: "Um hmm."

Guy: "Last night I read one."

FAHRENHEIT 451, 1966

290 His love is real. But he is not.

Child robot David is convinced that he will be made into a real human boy if only he can find the magical blue fairy from the story *Pinocchio*. In one poignant scene, he tells Gigolo Joe why he wants to be a real boy. "When I am real, Mommy's going to read to me and tuck me in my bed and sing to me and listen to what I say, and she will cuddle with me and tell me every day a hundred times a day that she loves me."

A.I.: ARTIFICIAL INTELLIGENCE, 2001

291 See you later

When you consider the age of this movie, it is incredible that it is still able to seduce us with its impressive technical and visual special effects. When the scientist (Claude Rains) strips off his facial bandages, dark glasses, gloves, wig, false nose, and all—yes, all—his clothing, everyone is amazed as he reveals himself to be completely invisible!

THE INVISIBLE MAN, 1933

292 It will have you sitting on the brink of eternity!

A technical malfunction in the Pentagon's strategic control system causes a false order to be sent to a B-58 squadron, instructing the bombers to fly beyond their fail-safe distance. At this point, the crew is trained to cease communications and prepare to fulfill its objective—bombing Moscow. The planes near their target, and the Americans and Soviets must decide to accept a final, desperate solution.

FAIL-SAFE, 1964

293 Every generation has a legend
Every journey has a first step
Every saga has a beginning

A door opens, and there stands Darth Maul, waiting.
"We'll handle this," declares Qui-Gon Jinn, and the two Jedis run to meet him. We all squirm in our seats because we know what's coming—one of the best swordfights in cinematic history.
All three warriors ceremoniously take off their robes and draw their light sabers, then go at it, two against one.

THE PHANTOM MENACE, 1999

294 They say there's nothing new under the sun. But under the ground…

Giant wormlike creatures burrow under the earth and pick off their human victims one by one in this cult comedy sci-fi movie. After his bomb shelter is destroyed when one of the creatures comes through the floor, survivalist and weapons expert Burt Gummer surveys his pride and joy one last time: "Food for five years, a thousand gallons of gas, air filtration, water filtration, Geiger counter. Bomb shelter! Underground…God damn monsters!"

TREMORS, 1990

295 How did it get here?

A group of scientists takes a block of ice from a crashed spacecraft back to their remote Arctic research station. Inside the ice is the spacecraft's frozen pilot. When the ice is accidentally allowed to melt, the scientists face a massive humanoid alien with killer instincts and a thirst for blood! In the most thrilling scene, the alien is doused with kerosene and set ablaze.

THE THING FROM ANOTHER WORLD, 1951

296 Watch what you say— it may come true!

In the year 2058, the earth is running out of air and drinking water, so the Robinson family embarks on a ten-year mission to the galaxy's only other planet whose habitat is similar to our own. At a media conference designed to stimulate hope, expedition leader John Robinson points at a map of the universe and jokes, "There's a lotta space out there to get lost in."

LOST IN SPACE, 1998

297 The ride of his life

Tommy Lee Jones lights up the sky in this tale of a group of elderly astronauts who undertake a space-flight mission to repair an ancient Russian satellite. While spacewalking, Jones and Clint Eastwood discover that the satellite's nuclear missiles are armed and aimed straight at the earth. Jones, who had never had the opportunity to make a moon landing, straps himself to the front of the deadly satellite and lines himself up for the moon.

SPACE COWBOYS, 2000

298 Something a little strange about Dad

Roy Neary heaps a huge dollop of mashed potatoes onto his plate… then another…and another. His family watches, incredulous, as he begins to obsessively sculpt the mound. Roy notices the looks on their faces. "Well, I guess you've noticed," he says. "Something's a little strange about Dad."

CLOSE ENCOUNTERS OF THE THIRD KIND, 1979

299 The story of a lifetime

Truman hasn't yet realized that he is the star of his own real-life TV show, but he is beginning to notice a few odd things—such as his wife randomly dropping product names into their conversations!

THE TRUMAN SHOW, 1998

300 The future of law enforcement

At a demonstration of the new anticrime robot ED-209, the robot develops a glitch. Young executive Mr. Kinney points his gun at it.
ED-209: "Please put down your weapon. You have 20 seconds to comply."
Dick Jones: "I think you'd better do as he says, Mr. Kinney."

ROBOCOP, 1987

Film Noir

Films noir are crime stories that are characterized by darkness—in terms of both theme and lighting. Their plots frequently involve a difficult choice to be made or a past mistake to clear up, but it's their mood, tone, and style that set these movies apart from other dramas. Films noir are moody, shadowy, and bleak, and their characters are often tinted with guilt, paranoia, and suspicion. The cynical heroes, or antiheroes, are often morally ambiguous, underworld figures, and the women either beautiful but deadly femmes fatales or "the only person a guy can trust." All of the characters are struggling to survive in a harsh and oppressive world.

Previous page: Orson Welles and Rita Hayworth in
The Lady from Shanghai (1948).

301 A story as explosive as his blazing automatics!

Police Detective Tom Polhaus lifts up the heavy black statuette as they are leaving the room, "It's heavy. What is it?" Private eye Sam Spade responds, while touching the bird, "The, uh, stuff that dreams are made of."

THE MALTESE FALCON, 1941

302 He's planting something and it isn't roses

Small-town bartender Ray is out in a barren field, trying to bury Marty, a mortally wounded Texas strip-club owner, alive!

BLOOD SIMPLE, 1984

303 There never was a woman like Gilda!

Rita Hayworth's slinky peformance of "Put the Blame on Mame" is perhaps the sexiest number ever to appear on film. As she performs it, we know that Glenn Ford is a helpless fly caught in her web.

GILDA, 1946

304 The truth is always in the last place you look

Limping con man "Verbal" Kint challenges the New York police: "You think you can catch Keyser Soze? You think a guy like that comes this close to getting caught, and sticks his head out? If he comes up for anything, it'll be to get rid of me. After that—my guess is you'll never hear from him again."

THE USUAL SUSPECTS, 1995

305 You can't kiss away a murder!

On the twelfth floor, Neff is clearly in pain. He staggers to his desk, bleeding from a gunshot wound, dying. He sits, lights a cigarette, and begins dictating into a machine: "I suppose you'll call this a confession when you hear it…Yes, I killed him. I killed him for money and for a woman. I didn't get the money and I didn't get the woman. Pretty, isn't it?"

DOUBLE INDEMNITY, 1944

306 "I told you...you know nothing about wickedness."

The shootout in the hall of mirrors is a legendary film-noir finale. O'Hara and the Bannisters shoot at multiple images of one another until the screen becomes kaleidoscopic with cracked and shattered glass, and tiny broken images of the characters.

THE LADY FROM SHANGHAI, 1948

307 Every kiss carved his name on another bullet

The alluring and treacherous femme fatale Kitty Collins confesses, "I'm poison—to myself and everybody around me."

THE KILLERS, 1946

308 Tough...Tense...Terrific...True!

Agents Dennis O'Brien and Tony Genaro have gone undercover in an attempt to bring a Detroit counterfeiting ring to justice. Everything seems to be going to plan until the harrowing scene in which O'Brien, who is still undercover, must watch helplessly as his partner Genaro is murdered.

T-MEN, 1947

309 A man—trying to run away from his past! A woman—trying to escape her future!

By a beautiful Sierra lake, Robert Mitchum is fishing while courting his sweet fiancée, Virginia Huston. She looks up at the sky and says, "They say the day you die, your name is written on a cloud."

OUT OF THE PAST, 1947

310 Who's to be trusted?

Gloria Grahame falls for war veteran Humphrey Bogart, who is prone to blackouts and has been linked to a woman's murder. He is convinced that he didn't do it, but she finds clues that he may have...

IN A LONELY PLACE, 1950

311 Why will a woman leave the man she loves for a man she hates?

Millie Baxter and her new husband, Paul, plan to reunite at a hotel, but he doesn't show. She learns that a man has been killed in one of the rooms—then her husband calls and asks to meet her secretly. Could he be the killer?

WHEN STRANGERS MARRY, 1944

312 Shadow boxing

Slanting shadows splash across Susan Lowell as she runs through tunnels under a boxing ring. She's being chased by two hit men, who have been hired by her lover to keep an eye on her. The men corner her. She steps out of the shadows, while they remain in them.

THE BIG COMBO, 1955

313 A mother's love leads to murder

The movie opens at the shadowy Beragon beach house, where a car is parked with its headlights on. A gun fires, and bullets shatter a mirror behind the victim. He slumps over and falls to the floor in front of a flickering fire in a dim room. A gun is tossed in front of him. With his dying breath he whispers, "Mildred!"

MILDRED PIERCE, 1945

314 A tale of self-deception

Hustler Harry Fabian's scheme to "get rich quick" as a sports promoter goes awry, and he's off running from the gangsters through dark alleys, warehouses, seedy nightclubs, and backrooms, desperately trying to escape an inevitable fate.

NIGHT AND THE CITY, 1950

315 One drink too many

Accountant Frank Bigelow wakes up sick after a night out drinking. He sees a doctor, who informs him that he has been poisoned and only has a few days left to live:

Dr. MacDonald: "I'll arrange for your admission to the hospital immediately. Of course, I'll have to notify the police. This is a case for Homicide."

Frank Bigelow: "Homicide?"

Dr. MacDonald: "I don't think you fully understand, Bigelow. You've been murdered."

D.O.A. 1949

316 The strangest vengeance ever planned

This Orson Welles classic begins with an incredible tracking shot; the camera follows a bomb being planted on a car, and then the car's route through town. In one movement, the camera swoops through the squalid streets as a Mexican detective (Charlton Heston) and his American wife (Janet Leigh) walk across the U.S. border— right up until the moment the bomb explodes and a man is killed.

TOUCH OF EVIL, 1958

317 He'll have you in a dither with his zither

Harry Lime (Orson Welles) appears in this film for no more than fifteen minutes, yet his are probably the most memorable scenes of all. In one, he confronts Holly Martins (Joseph Cotten) in a car on top of the world-famous Austrian ferris wheel, the Riesenrad, and puts some cruelly difficult questions to him: "Would you feel any pity if one of those dots stopped moving forever? If I said you could have twenty-thousand pounds for every dot that stops, would you really, old man, tell me to keep my money without hesitation?"

THE THIRD MAN, 1949

318 "My name's Marlowe"

Marlowe meets one of the general's two alluring daughters—the young, troubled, errant, frequently doped-up nymphomaniac heiress Carmen, who greets him wearing a white polka-dot miniskirt. He notices her legs as she descends the stairs. The capricious girl tells him, "You're not very tall, are you?" "Well, I, uh, I try to be" is all he can manage to say in reply.

THE BIG SLEEP, 1946

319 She lived two amazing lives!

Joan Ellis is suffering from a split-personality disorder. She subjects herself to hypnosis to try to rid herself of her evil alter ego—the one that may have killed her boyfriend!

BEWITCHED, 1945

320 You could hear a pin drop

In an entire scene of tense silence, thieves disable an alarm system and crack a safe. They don't utter a single world, and we hear only the muffled sound of a chisel being hit and a single, loud note from a piano that is accidentally struck. Then, the moment they get safely home, the thieves triumphantly break into song.

RIFIFI, 1954

321 Police baffled by the faceless killer!

Police detectives have constructed a mannequin of a murderer called "The Judge" from witness descriptions, and they talk to it, revealing all their frustrations. As they leave the room, the figure slowly begins to move...It's the real "Judge" and he has heard everything!

FOLLOW ME QUIETLY, 1949

322 Time is running out

Catherine goes off to meet her husband, Kirk Bennett, who has been falsely sentenced for murder and is scheduled to die the next morning. Meanwhile, her fellow amateur sleuth Martin Blair slips into an alcoholic stupor, just before the real killer is revealed.
BLACK ANGEL, 1946

323 A double double cross

After accomplishing his latest job, assassin Alan Ladd reports to Willard Gates to collect his $1000 fee. He soon discovers that the money is marked—he has been double-crossed by Gates and his boss Alvin Brewster, who is trying to tie up all his loose ends.
THIS GUN FOR HIRE, 1942

324 Like the boy who cried, "Wolf!"

Young Tommy Woodry, a boy with a reputation for lying, has seen his neighbors commit a murder, but when he tries to tell his parents and the police, they don't believe him. In one scene, they actually force the little witness to confront the killers and apologize for the awful things he's been saying about them!
THE WINDOW, 1949

325 "There are things you do hate, Lord."

In a strip joint, avenging "preacher" Robert Mitchum is watching a stripper, who arouses him. He grabs the switchblade from his coat pocket, exposing the letters H-A-T-E, which are tattooed on his knuckles. As his passion rises, the switchblade is flicked open. "There are too many of them. Can't kill the world."

THE NIGHT OF THE HUNTER, 1955

326 Can he crack his habit?

Bob is a good-mannered and well-respected reformed bank robber, but he is tempted to consider one final heist when an old friend, who is working as a casino croupier, reveals where a huge haul is locked away in a safe.

BOB THE GAMBLER, 1955

327 A deadly whirlpool of intrigue...

Private eye Mike Hammer picks up a woman stranded on a back road wearing only a trench coat, with nothing underneath. Someone runs them off the road. As he lies semiconscious, he sees the woman being tortured and killed. The mercenary Hammer smells the potential to earn some cash—if he can only unravel what's going on!

KISS ME DEADLY, 1955

328 "She's trouble, Ned. Real big-time, major-league trouble."

Matty, killed in an explosion, has been identified by dental records. Ned is imprisoned for her murder. Ned looks in Matty's high-school yearbook and finds out that she is, in reality, Mary Ann Simpson, whose ambition was: "to be rich and live in an exotic land." The movie cuts to a final shot of a very much alive Matty relaxing on a beautiful beach…

BODY HEAT, 1981

329 He's Ma's little boy

Cody feels a severe pain in his head as he's loading a gun. He winces, groans, and keels over—and the gun goes off as he lands. His mother, Verna, steers him to the bedroom, where we catch her soothing him as he sits on her lap.
Verna: "It's his second one he's had in a month."
Big Ed: "He's nuts, just like his old man."

WHITE HEAT, 1949

330 Making waves

Gumshoe Mark McPherson inspects writer Waldo Lydecker's apartment. The writer calls McPherson to join him in the bathroom, where Lydecker is reclining in his pool-sized bathtub, his modesty covered only by his typewriter. McPherson: "Nice little place you have here, Lydecker." Lydecker: "It's lavish, but I call it home."

LAURA, 1944

331 "I brought you nightmares."

As this brilliant Hitchcock thriller ends, young Charlie and the audience are left with Uncle Charlie's grim spoken memorial: "You wake up every morning of your life and you know perfectly well that there's nothing in the world to trouble you. You go through your ordinary little day, and at night you sleep your untroubled, ordinary little sleep filled with peaceful, stupid dreams. And I brought you nightmares."

SHADOW OF A DOUBT, 1943

332 Their love was a flame that destroyed!

With the "Dear John" note to Nick in the cash register, Cora and Frank walk away from the café to hitchhike on the highway.

Cora: "Too bad Nick took the car."

Frank: "Even if the car were here, we couldn't take it, not unless we want to spend the first night in jail. Stealing a man's wife, that's nothing. But stealing his car, that's larceny."

THE POSTMAN ALWAYS RINGS TWICE, 1946

333 He went searching for love…but fate forced a detour to revelry…violence…mystery!

Al Roberts thumbs a ride with a businessman, who complains about his last passenger, a frantic woman who scratched him… then he mysteriously dies. Roberts panics and, fearing he may be accused of murder, throws the body into the desert and drives away. But then he picks up his own hitchhiker—a bad-tempered redhead who recognizes the car!

DETOUR, 1945

334 She's a midnight gal in a nine o'clock town

Desperate for wealth, Rosa Moline complains, "If I don't get out of here, I'll just die! Living here is like waiting for the funeral to begin. No, it's like waiting in the coffin for them to take you out!"

BEYOND THE FOREST, 1949

335 What dreams may come...

Mike Ward falls asleep and dreams that he has been arrested for murder. When he awakes, he runs next door and finds that his neighbor's throat has been slashed—and the police think he did it.

STRANGER ON THE THIRD FLOOR, 1940

336 Don't paint yourself into a corner

Christopher Cross thinks he has rescued the beautiful Kitty March from a dangerous thug when he meets her in a dark alley, but the thug was actually her pimp boyfriend. Cross is an ordinary man, but he passes himself off as a successful and wealthy artist, and she takes an immediate interest in him.

SCARLET STREET, 1945

337 Burglar ballet

A group of thieves expertly weave their way through a crowd at a railway station like a swarm of locusts. They work together to swiftly and silently relieve the unsuspecting people of their wallets, in a scene that reminds us all to be far more careful with our belongings.

PICKPOCKET, 1959

338 To be expected...

In typical film noir style, a private detective, who has been approached by a wealthy executive to stop a blackmail scam against him, becomes the target of the blackmailers himself—even though he hasn't decided to take the job yet!

BLACKMAIL, 1947

339 Put them all together, they spell M-U-R-D-E-R!

A reporter agrees to incriminate himself in a murder case to help his editor, who is pursuing a campaign against capital punishment. They plant evidence and pose for photographs that will prove his innocence. But things suddenly go very wrong when the only man who can exonerate him is killed in a car accident...

BEYOND A REASONABLE DOUBT, 1956

340 There is more than one way to kill a man!

Two smartly dressed assassins enter a college for the blind. They threaten a sightless receptionist, locate their victim, break into his office, and coolly shoot him. One assassin is left wondering why the victim didn't run, but simply stood and waited to die. The other has a theory: "There's only one guy who's not afraid to die; that's a guy who's already dead."

THE KILLERS, 1964

341 A promising career goes down the drain

A psychopathic burglar (Richard Basehart) stays one step ahead of the police by monitoring their radio communications and changing his methods to put them off the scent. They finally manage to catch up with him and, in a stylish predecessor to the famous chase in *The Third Man*, chase him through the Los Angeles sewer system.

HE WALKED BY NIGHT, 1948

342 Two-fisted, hardboiled, terrific!

A dark, lonely road. Close-up on Marlowe's face. A slight noise—he casts a quick sideways glance but is felled from behind by an unseen assailant. "The sap caught me just behind the ear. A large black pool opened beneath my feet and I dived right in. It had no bottom. When I came round I felt like an amputated leg!"

MURDER, MY SWEET, 1945

343 Some memories are best forgotten

The movie opens with a shot of a hand holding a Polaroid of a murder scene. The photo slowly un-develops, fading to black, then we see a murder played out in rewind—the victim's blood seeps up a wall and back into the wound; the bullet cartridges spin back into the barrel of a gun. The murder is erased.

MEMENTO, 2000

344 A hard cop and a soft dame!

Even though we don't actually see it happening, the moment in which the raging Stone flings a pot of scalding coffee into his girlfriend's face is appallingly memorable—"My face! My face!"

THE BIG HEAT, 1953

345 There's nothing more deadly than a gentle man pushed too far

Captain Harry Morgan charters his fishing boat to four men in an effort to pay off his debts. Once out to sea, things take a turn for the worse when he discovers that they are criminals on the run and a deadly gunfight breaks out.

THE BREAKING POINT, 1950

346 He bought the farm

The Asphalt Jungle ends with one of the greatest finales in film history as the mortally wounded Dix (Sterling Hayden) flees, delirious, from the police to a farm in the Kentucky countryside where he was raised.

THE ASPHALT JUNGLE, 1950

347 It's a family affair

Jake Gittes's patience has run out. He is going to get answers about the young woman that Evelyn Mulwray is hiding from him even if he has to knock them out of her. "She's my daughter." He slaps her. "My sister." He slaps her again. "She's my daughter." And again. "She's my sister and my daughter!"

CHINATOWN, 1974

348 Contemporary film noir

A supermodel, wearing a diamond-covered gown worth millions of dollars, is at the Cannes Film Festival. A photographer named Laure seduces her and strategically undresses her in the bathroom, where Laure's accomplices are waiting to switch the diamond dress with a replica covered in cut glass.

FEMME FATALE, 2002

349 Double dame trouble!

Johnny Morrison returns home from World War II to discover that his wife has been unfaithful. A fierce fight breaks out, and he is tempted to pull out his gun, but instead he strides off into the rain, leaving his weapon behind. Johnny is then picked up by the ex-wife of the man *his* wife has been having the affair with.

THE BLUE DAHLIA, 1946

350 Left with egg on his face

Carnival operator Tyrone Power gradually loses control of the show and begins his fascinatingly dark, downward spiral to the lowest skids, where we find him playing a sideshow geek who bites the heads off of live chickens.

NIGHTMARE ALLEY, 1947

Thrillers

Thrillers are relentless films that have us on the edge of our seats as tension builds to a thrilling climax. The formula is fairly universal—the central characters are put into mysterious or deadly situations, or people's lives are threatened by strange and sinister forces. These movies are crammed with villains and victims, terrorists, cops, psychopaths, criminals, and secret agents. Excitement and suspense are key. With murders, conspiracies, chases, politics, and romance thrown in, these are the films to turn to when we need a good rush of adrenaline!

Previous page: A scene from *The Birds* (1963).

351 Hunted... by a thousand men! Haunted... by a lovely girl!

Pulp-fiction writer Holly Martins arrives through a cloud of train steam, hoping for the job promised by the elusive Harry Lime. He makes his way to Lime's apartment, walking under a ladder en route. When he arrives, he can only stare as an elderly tenant shouts at him in incomprehensible German. Then the zither strikes up the famous theme.

THE THIRD MAN, 1949

352 Quid pro quo

Infamous serial killer Hannibal Lecter has not seen a woman for some time when FBI rookie Clarice Starling is sent to question him. Lecter is safely locked away behind thick glass, but his nostrils taste the air like some hunting python, and he perceptively says "You use Evyan skin cream, and sometimes you wear L'Air du Temps, but not today."

THE SILENCE OF THE LAMBS, 1991

353 Bullitt—some other kind of cop. Pity the guy he works for.

The scene that wins hands down as being the most spectacular is the ten-minute car chase. Lieutenant Bullitt, in a '68 Ford Mustang GT, and the hit men, in a '68 Dodge Charger, were filmed with handheld cameras as they raced through the streets of San Francisco.

BULLITT, 1968

354 If they survive…will we?

Holocaust survivor and Nazi hunter Ezra Lieberman suddenly discovers, to his horror, that Dr. Josef Mengele has cloned 94 young Hitlers!

THE BOYS FROM BRAZIL, 1978

355 Today, only a handful of people know what it means…Soon you will know.

There's been an accident at a nuclear power plant, and the management is trying to cover it up. In the dramatic final scene, Jack Lemmon barricades himself in the control room of the nuclear reactor in a desperate attempt to try to broadcast the truth.

THE CHINA SYNDROME, 1979

356 A murdered wife. A one-armed man. An obsessed detective. The chase begins.

There are several striking chase sequences in this film, but no one will forget the potentially lethal dive that fugitive Dr. Richard Kimble takes from a dam down into a cascading waterfall below.

THE FUGITIVE, 1993

357 "Is it safe?"

Marathon runner Dustin Hoffman is ruthlessly interrogated by Nazi dentist Laurence Olivier over some diamonds. Olivier rigs together a dentist's apparatus and starts drilling Hoffman's teeth without any anesthetic, while relentlessly asking him, "Is it safe?"

MARATHON MAN, 1976

358 "Haven't you ever needed someone?"

Bob Hoskins is the gangland lad responsible for the welfare of lovely hooker Cathy Tyson. In one scene, after she gives him money to smarten himself up, he turns up looking ridiculous. She takes him shopping, and she selects a style that suits his position.

MONA LISA, 1986

359 Electric tension!

Hitchcock used an innovative technique to sidestep the "three-second rule" regarding on-screen kisses, and this film offers up the longest kiss ever seen at the time. It was achieved by not making it a single kiss—Cary Grant and Ingrid Bergman kiss, nibble, and caress while talking, answering the telephone, and moving around the apartment. The camera follows them in one continuous shot, and they never leave one another's embrace.

NOTORIOUS, 1946

360 An assassin on the loose. A president in danger. Only one man stands between them...

Menacing hit man Mitch Leary has built a pistol that is undetectable by metal detectors and is trying it out in the marshes, when a hunter sees him:

Hunter: That's a cool gun you got there....What's it made of?"
Leary: "Composite. Like plastic."
Hunter: "You wouldn't want to sell it would you?"
Leary: "No, I need it....To assassinate the president."
The hunter laughs nervously, then Leary turns and swiftly shoots him.

IN THE LINE OF FIRE, 1993

361 "I won't be ignored!"

An obsessed woman (Glenn Close) terrorizes the philandering lawyer (Michael Douglas) who had a one-night stand with her and then returned to his wife. In an unforgettable scene, he comes home to find a cooking pot on the stove—with the family's pet rabbit boiling inside it!

FATAL ATTRACTION, 1987

362 We'll be listening to you

A skilled sound engineer (Gene Hackman) is employed by a mysterious figure to record a young couple talking in a noisy public square. From one line of their conversation, he becomes convinced that someone's out to kill them, until the pivotal moment when he cleans up the recording and hears the vital inflection that he'd missed before: "He'd kill *us* if he got the chance."

THE CONVERSATION, 1974

363 Flesh seduces. Passion kills.

Police interrogators sit before attractive murder-suspect Sharon Stone. She smokes, even though they tell her she can't: "What are you going to do? Charge me with smoking?" She directs her attention to cop Michael Douglas: "Have you ever f***ed on cocaine, Nick? It's nice." Then she uncrosses, opens, and recrosses her legs, revealing that she's panty-free.

BASIC INSTINCT, 1992

364 Falsely accused. Wrongly imprisoned. He fought for justice to clear his father's name.

The Irishmen wrongfully arrested for IRA bombings in 1974 have their charges dismissed. One of them, Gerard Conlon, whose father died in prison, pronounces, "I'm a free man, and I'm going out the front door." Once out, he lets it be known that he'll continue to fight, "in the name of my father and of the truth."

IN THE NAME OF THE FATHER, 1993

365 A murderer would never parade his crime in front of an open window

The most suspenseful scene in this classic Hitchcock thriller is that of Grace Kelly searching the suspected murderer's apartment. James Stewart sees the man returning home, but can only watch, powerless in his wheelchair from his rear window...

REAR WINDOW, 1954

366 Loyalty is bought; betrayal is a way of life...

Robert De Niro and Jean Reno pursue their target through Paris during the rush hour, in what becomes one of the most epic car chases ever filmed.

RONIN, 1998

367 Never monotonous

John Gielgud and Peter Lorre are in Switzerland to kill an enemy agent in this World War I thriller. They hear a single note coming from a deserted church. As they approach, Lorre produces a knife and grips his hat between his teeth to free his hands. They discover that the organist is a corpse, who is slumped across the keyboard.

SECRET AGENT, 1936

368 You'll never go in the water again!

Two young lovers find a secluded spot on the beach. The girl strips and goes into the ocean, while the boy struggles to undress and join her. All seems peaceful and romantic, but then the music starts—two notes played over and over, becoming progressively more frantic on deep strings. The girl disappears—a great white shark has taken her!

JAWS, 1975

369 The wedding night, the anticipation, the kiss, the knife, but above all…the suspense!

Creepy Robert Mitchum is an evil preacher with "Love" and "Hate" tattooed on his hands. He is obsessed with finding $10,000 hidden by a condemned convict. He's already married and murdered the dead convict's wife and he now turns to her two children, in a terrifying scene in which they flee from him into a swamp.

THE NIGHT OF THE HUNTER, 1955

370 Sister, sister, oh so fair, why is there blood all over your hair?

Aging Jane Hudson is garishly dressed up as the little-girl starlet she once was. While her sister is imprisoned upstairs, she is being coached for her comeback by her newly appointed musical director, Edwin Flagg, and she croaks out her most famous song: "I've written a letter to Daddy; his address is Heaven above…"

WHAT EVER HAPPENED TO BABY JANE? 1962

371 Not for honor. Not for country. For his wife and child.

After Jack Ryan spoils the attempted assassination of a member of the royal family in London, an IRA splinter group targets him and his family—hospitalizing his daughter. Jack meets with Paddy O'Neil, an IRA official, to ask for his help:

Jack Ryan: "I want to know where Sean Miller and Kevin O'Donnell are."

Paddy O'Neil: "Let me try and understand this. You want me to sell out my fellow Irishman to you? Is that why you came down here? You don't understand me at all."

Jack Ryan: "Oh, I think I do."

PATRIOT GAMES, 1992

372 "We all meet death somewhere along the way."

Vulnerable American heiress Kit Preston strolls through a thick London fog and is stalked by a mysterious, eerie voice that threatens to kill her: "Mrs. Preston, I'm over here! Don't be afraid, Mrs. Preston. I'm close to you. Close enough to reach out—and put my hands around your neck, Mrs. Preston!"

MIDNIGHT LACE, 1960

373 Eight-year-old Samuel: sole witness to a murder. Three killers who'll stop at nothing to silence him. One honest cop who'll give his life to save him...

The young Amish boy who witnessed a murder is looking around the police station when he spots a photograph. He sees the killer's face among a group of faces. Cop Harrison Ford comes over to see what he's looking at, and the boy identifies the killer—another cop!

WITNESS, 1985

374 The thrill spectacle of the year!

The most spectacular scene in this movie is one of pandemonium aboard a transoceanic airplane. Filmed over the shoulders of the two pilots, we see the plane ditching into the ocean. Water quickly fills the cabin as it hits, leaving the passengers struggling for air as they try to escape the flooded plane.

FOREIGN CORRESPONDENT, 1940

375 He's out to get even

To look at him, William Foster seems like a normal sort of guy, but in a traffic jam on the hottest day of the year he abandons his car on the road and begins walking into an urban nightmare: "I'm going home."

FALLING DOWN, 1993

376 "Come along, Mrs. Thornhill."

The cliff-dangling scene is a great moment of suspense, as Eve and Roger cling onto the huge stone faces of Mount Rushmore for their very lives. Roger reaches out, grabs Eve, and—thanks to a great piece of editing—pulls her up into the berth of a train's sleeping car.

NORTH BY NORTHWEST, 1959

377 The newest attorney at the world's most powerful law firm has never lost a case. But he's about to lose his soul.

High above New York on the rooftop of an immense skyscraper, the devil (Al Pacino) negotiates with a ruthless young attorney from Florida (Keanu Reeves)—seducing him with offers of power, fame, and fortune.

DEVIL'S ADVOCATE, 1997

378 "I'll never tell."

A New York psychiatrist (Michael Douglas) is locked in a tense battle of wills—the troubled teenage girl before him has locked a six-digit number away in her subconscious, and that number is the key to saving his kidnapped daughter. He desparately tries every trick he knows to coax it out of her, but the clock is ticking.

DON'T SAY A WORD, 2001

379 See them all in a film about fantasy. And reality. Vice. And versa.

A gangster (James Fox) on the run takes refuge in the house of a rock musician (Mick Jagger), who wants to find out all about him. Jagger feeds Fox a magic mushroom to loosen him up a bit, sending him on quite a trip: "I need a bohemian atmosphere!"

PERFORMANCE, 1970

380 The scream you hear may be your own!

Cool-talking, Californian DJ Dave picks up the seductive Evelyn Draper at a bar and takes her for a one-night stand, unaware that she is the listener who regularly asks him to "play 'Misty' for me, Dave."

"PLAY MISTY FOR ME," 1971

381 The most bizarre bank siege ever

Al Pacino tries to rob a bank to fund a sex-change operation for his male lover, but gets trapped inside it with his dim-witted sidekick and eight hostages. In one great scene, he goes outside the bank and starts throwing money to the assembled crowd, who cheer him like a hero, while he shouts "Attica! Attica!"

DOG DAY AFTERNOON, 1975

382 Four men ride a wild river. A weekend turns into a nightmare.

We know things are going to turn nasty when a couple of degenerate mountain men hold Ned Beatty at gunpoint, making him strip—and squeal like a pig!

DELIVERANCE, 1972

383 Jack in a box

In a memorably expressionistic finale, black-bobbed prostitute Lulu becomes the tragic victim of Jack the Ripper on the dark streets of London.

PANDORA'S BOX, 1929

384 Cover-up!

As left-wing, antinuclear politician Yves Montand walks across a square to jeers from a fascist mob, a three-wheeled truck bears down on him. An assassin stands on the truck's flatbed and strikes him one mighty blow to the head with a wooden weapon before stealing off into the night.

Z, 1969

385 Play at your own risk

IRA soldier Fergus kisses the gorgeous hairdresser Dil, and she slowly lets her robe fall to the floor. The camera moves with it, and we suddenly see that she's a *he*. Fergus reacts suddenly and runs out of the room: "Jesus. I feel sick." Dil simply says, "I'm sorry…I thought you knew."

THE CRYING GAME, 1992

386 "Come into my parlor," said the spider to the fly.

An obsessed and insane man wants to become as famous as a notorious murderer from the 1930s, so he kidnaps a senator's daughter. He chooses a worthy adversary—retired detective-turned-writer Alex Cross (Morgan Freeman), who will guarantee that his crime is well documented. He places a vital piece of evidence into Cross's mailbox, thereby inextricably drawing the writer into the plot.

ALONG CAME A SPIDER, 2001

387 He was young, handsome, a millionaire—and he'd just pulled off the perfect crime! She was young, beautiful, a super sleuth—sent to investigate it!

Steve McQueen, as a thief with a taste for the good life, sits down with Faye Dunaway, the insurance investigator who's out to catch him, and the pair play the steamiest game of chess ever!

THE THOMAS CROWN AFFAIR, 1968

388 Handcuffed to the girl who double-crossed him

Pamela awakens in the night while Hannay is sleeping and slips free from the handcuffs. She sneaks out of the room and, overhearing two spies talking downstairs, is shocked to hear proof of Hannay's innocence. Just before the landlord can give them away, his wife comes in and shoos the spies away for drinking after hours. Then she smiles at her husband: "You old fool, you wouldn't have given away a young couple, would ya?"

THE 39 STEPS, 1935

389 A psychic thriller

John Baxter and his wife are living in Venice, trying to get over the death of their daughter, who drowned while wearing a shiny red raincoat. A blind medium tells them that their daughter is trying to contact them. Then Baxter sees a little figure in red running alongside the canals, and he follows it into the shadows…

DON'T LOOK NOW, 1973

390 Unlock the secret

After discovering that the Nazis have changed the "Enigma Code," that commands their U-boats, Tom Jericho has to put his talented brain to work and race against time to crack the new code. It is a painfully slow process, and, as he collects the signals he needs to work from, his colleagues get anxious that he is not making enough progress:

Tom Jericho: "Seventeen signals—it's not enough yet."

Cave: "Well, why the hell not?!"

Tom Jericho: "When I'm done, we'll be looking for a needle in a haystack. But if we stop now, it'll be a hundred thousand haystacks."

ENIGMA, 2001

187

391 Fear is the driving force

David Mann is locked in a battle of wits and speed with a demonic tanker truck on America's loneliest back roads. In one scene, he tries to outrun the truck up a steep hill, but his engine begins to boil over, and he literally begs the car to keep going: "You can't beat me on the grade. You can't beat me on the grade!"

DUEL, 1971

392 Branching out...

Edward Fox buys a watermelon and goes out into the country. He uses a knife to stick the watermelon to a tree in a net bag, adjusts his newly fabricated assassin's rifle, then blows the poor piece of fruit to smithereens—just as he intends to do to President de Gaulle.

THE DAY OF THE JACKAL, 1973

393 What would you do?

When Jeff and Amy Taylor's car breaks down on an isolated road, they are pleased to accept the assistance of a friendly truck driver, who drives Amy to a diner to phone for help. Jeff manages to get the car started himself while they are gone, but when he reaches the diner there is no sign of his wife—no one has seen her or the trucker!

BREAKDOWN, 1997

394 Who's your tailor?

Suspected saboteur Barry Kane corners fifth columnist Frank Fry on the torch of the Statue of Liberty. Fry loses his balance and falls over the railing, clinging to the statue's hand. Kane attempts to save Fry by gripping at his jacket sleeve, but the seam tears, and Fry's life hangs by a thread.

SABOTEUR, 1942

395 Waxing lyrical

Tough guy Pinkie Brown (Richard Attenborough) is nagged by his date to go into a recording booth to cut a message for her. While she waits outside, unable to hear, he lays it on the record—a scathing diatribe on how much he despises her.

BRIGHTON ROCK, 1947

396 A story of love and redemption

Eunice obsessively travels the highways of northern England, searching for a woman named Judith and the name of an unknown melody that is stuck in her mind. In one scene, she asks the cashier at a filling station to help her recognize the song, then accuses her of being Judith. When the cashier denies this, Eunice kills her.

BUTTERFLY KISS, 1995

397 The birds are coming

Handsome bachelor attorney Mitch mistakes Melanie for a salesclerk in the pet store and they both flirt while discussing a pair of lovebirds:

Mitch: "Well, these are for my sister, for her birthday, see, and uh, as she's only going to be eleven…I…I wouldn't want a pair of birds that were too demonstrative."

Melanie: "I understand completely."

Mitch: "At the same time, I wouldn't want them to be too aloof, either."

Melanie: "No, of course not."

Mitch: "Do you happen to have a pair of birds that are just friendly?"

THE BIRDS, 1963

398 Copycat burglar

After a string of copycat burglaries by someone using his trademark, notorious thief John Robie, alias Smith, meets with insurance agent H. H. Hughson. Robie asks for a list of the company's richest clients, so he can try to get the stolen jewels back and clear his name: "I take all the risks. You get all the jewelry back." Hughson comments, "Mr. Smith. It strikes me that only an honest man would be so foolish."

TO CATCH A THIEF, 1955

399 Power can be murder to resist

Mitchell McDeere's life is on the line—he knows too much, and it seems as through everyone is after him. His only hope is to convince a top mob boss that he is not a threat, while providing himself with a safety net. Mitch arrives just as the mobsters are discussing how to get rid of him:

Tommie Morolto: "If only I could get my hands on this kid."

Ruth: "I think it's urgent, Mr. Morolto."

Tommie Morolto: "Ruth thinks it's urgent, Joey. What do you think?"

Ruth: "It's a Mr. McDeere. Mr. Mitchell McDeere. He's waiting to see you."

Joey Morolto: "I think Ruth is right."

THE FIRM, 1993

400 Something strange is happening in the town of Stepford

The "perfect" wives in Stepford all seem to be obsessed with housekeeping. Bobbie, the sassy new woman in the neighborhood, comments that it's like a competition, "and the housewife with the neatest place gets Robert Redford for Christmas."

THE STEPFORD WIVES, 1975

Crime

For decades we've delighted in watching every conceivable combination of cops and robbers, detectives and criminals, and special agents and gangsters battling it out. Crime films are the places to find tough guys, beautiful women, fast cars, and lots of guns! The characters are usually struggling to acquire power, wealth, or revenge, or to prevent someone else from getting them. From the classic gangsters of the '30s and '40s to the reckless cops of the '70s and '80s to today's new breed of violent criminals, when it comes to memorable moments, these movies are guaranteed not to let us down.

Previous page: Sidney Poitier and Rod Steiger in
In the Heat of the Night (1967).

401 "Whaddya hear? Whaddya say?"

Gangster Rocky asks his old friend Jerry how he decided to become a priest. Jerry tells him that he received his calling while riding on a bus past a cathedral and Rocky remarks, "That's funny. I got an idea on top of a bus one time. Got me six years."

ANGELS WITH DIRTY FACES, 1938

402 Dirty Harry is at it again!

Harry Callahan saves a hostage and prevents a robbery at his local coffee shop by pointing his Magnum handgun at the armed robber and taunting him with the immortal line, "Go ahead, make my day."

SUDDEN IMPACT, 1983

403 A homespun murder story

In snow-covered North Dakota, police chief Marge Gunderson slowly edges her way around a lakeside cabin and discovers Grimsrud feeding Showalter's leg into the wood chipper.

FARGO, 1996

404 An epic tale of crime and obsession and two men on opposite sides of the law

The diner conversation between Al Pacino (as Vincent Hanna) and Robert De Niro (as Neil McCauley) is the highlight of this movie, not only because it marks the first time that these two legends shared the screen together, but also because it reveals how much the cop and the criminal have in common:

McCauley: "Maybe we should both be doing something else, pal."

Hanna: "I don't know how to do anything else."

McCauley: "Neither do I."

Hanna: "I don't much want to either."

McCauley: "Neither do I."

HEAT, 1995

405 What happens when a professional killer violates the code? Get Carter!

Gangster Jack Carter is in Newcastle looking for his brother's murderer when two local heavies break into his hotel and threaten him. Carter immediately takes the upper hand, grabbing his shotgun and chasing them outside—completely naked.

GET CARTER, 1971

406 "They got a murder on their hands."

Redneck Sheriff Gillespie, who is heading a racially motivated murder, confronts the African-American detective sent to assist him:

Gillespie: "Well, you're pretty sure of yourself, ain't you, Virgil. Virgil, that's a funny name for a nigger boy that comes from Philadelphia. What do they call you up there?"

Virgil: "They call me Mister Tibbs."

IN THE HEAT OF THE NIGHT, 1967

407 Stealing, cheating, killing. Who said romance is dead?

In an epic face-off, ex-cop Dennis Hopper stands up to debonair Sicilian gangster Christopher Walken when he comes looking for his son. Hopper knows he's about to die, so he accepts the beating he is given, smiles, and then coolly insults Walken's Sicilian heritage while puffing on a cigarette.

TRUE ROMANCE, 1993

197

408 "Don't ask me about my business."

This film is a treasure chest of amazing scenes and moments, but one of the most poignant comes near the end of the film, when Michael Corleone overcomes his pangs of conscience and closes the door on his wife to become "The Godfather."

THE GODFATHER, 1972

409 Off the record, on the q.t., and very hush-hush...

During the interrogation of an alleged rapist, cop Bud White bursts into the room and pulls out his gun. He empties all but one bullet, then sticks the gun into the suspect's mouth and menacingly threatens, "One in six—where's the girl?"

L.A. CONFIDENTIAL, 1997

410 "You want me, you're going to have to come and get me!"

Wannabe-gangster Rico shares his dream to be a "Big Man" with his best friend, Joe: "Yeah, money's all right, but it ain't everything. Yeah, I'll be somebody. Look hard at a bunch of guys and know that they'll do anything you tell 'em. Have your own way or nothin'. Be somebody."

LITTLE CAESAR, 1930

411 "I've been upstairs with your boss, shooting the breeze…shooting his fish."

Sergeant Martin Riggs sneaks into the South African embassy and confronts Arjen Rudd in his office. Riggs knows the diplomat can't be touched, so he causes mayhem by shooting Rudd's aquarium, filling the room with water and flailing fish.

LETHAL WEAPON 2, 1989

412 "I understand what I see in him. The truth about us all."

When IRA leader Johnny McQueen is wounded in a robbery attempt, he is left to evade the police alone. As he wanders deliriously through Belfast, he has unforgettably vivid hallucinations of faces from the past in the bubbles of his beer and of paintings flying off a wall.

ODD MAN OUT, 1947

413 "All that Cain did to Abel was to murder him."

Wall Street lawyer Joe Morse slowly descends a great stone staircase to find his estranged brother dead and dumped on the rocks next to the Hudson River lighthouse: "It was like going down to the bottom of the world."

FORCE OF EVIL, 1948

414

"We are the self-preservation society…"

Michael Caine's crew have just stolen $4 million worth of gold bullion, and they're trying to make their getaway during an international soccer match between Italy and England. With an exceptionally planned traffic jam, the beautiful city of Turin, three Mini Coopers in red, white, and blue, and an unforgettable soundtrack, we are treated to one of the best car chases in cinema history!

THE ITALIAN JOB, 1969

415 Look in your heart!

In a crucial scene, mobster Tommy Reagan leads double-crossing bookmaker Bernie Bernbaum through the trees to an isolated spot at Miller's Crossing. As Reagan prepares to shoot him, Bernie pleads for his life: "I can't die out here in the woods like a dumb animal!…You can't kill me. I'm praying to you! Look in your heart!" But will Reagan listen to his heart, or his head?

MILLER'S CROSSING, 1990

416 There are bad cops and there are good cops—and then there's Bullitt

In a small, seedy hotel room, two cops discuss the brutal murder of an important witness in protective custody:
Captain Bennett: "He let the killers in himself? Why would he do a thing like that?"
Frank Bullitt: [sarcastically] "I'm waiting to ask him."

BULLITT, 1968

417 Joe is still alive!

Katherine Grant sees her innocent fiancé, Joe Wilson, trapped behind flaming jail bars in a prison that has been set on fire by an angry mob. "I could smell myself burn," he says later.

FURY, 1936

418 40 stories of sheer adventure!

In one fantastic scene, John McClane runs across the roof of the 40-story Nakatomi building, ties the hose from a nearby fire reel around his waist, says "Oh, god, please don't let me die!" and jumps—just as Hans Gruber hits the detonator and the building explodes.

DIE HARD, 1988

419 "We all make mistakes...That's why they put the rubber on the ends of pencils."

Wealthy, sinister gangster Baby Face Martin returns to his old East River neighborhood in New York City. He meets his mother in a slum, and she gives him a tremendous slap across the face—but not before she's called him a dirty yellow dog and a no good tramp!

DEAD END, 1937

420 "I have to obey it!"

In one suspenseful scene, a young girl bounces her ball against a post with a newspaper pasted on it that reads: "Who is the Murderer?" and that offers a reward for the capture of a child killer. Then the shadow of a man falls over her...

M, 1931

421 A guy without a conscience!

Private detective Sam Spade impassively phones his secretary when he is told about his partner's death: "Now Effie. It's me...Now listen, Precious. Miles has been shot...Yeah, dead. Now don't get excited...Now, you'll have to break the news to Iva. I'd fry for it...And keep her away from me..."

THE MALTESE FALCON, 1941

202

422 He's a lonely, forgotten man desperate to prove that he's alive

Travis Bickle, an alienated psychotic cab driver on a mission to clean up the scum on the streets of New York, constructs a quick-draw device from the drawer runners of an old desk and tries it out in front of the mirror. Squaring up to his own reflection, he asks, "You talkin' to me? Then who the hell else…You talkin' to me?" Then, with a flick of the wrist, his gun suddenly appears in his hand.

TAXI DRIVER, 1976

423 The media made them superstars

In the shocking ending to this ultraviolent movie, the two young serial killers, Mickey and Mallory Knox, shoot Wayne Gale, the TV reporter who made them famous, live on camera.

Mickey: "I realized my true calling in life."

Wayne Gale: "What's that?"

Mickey: "Shit, man, I'm a natural born killer."

NATURAL BORN KILLERS, 1994

424 Thank God, it's Friday!

When Sergeant Friday (Dan Aykroyd) is interviewing Sylvia Wiss (Julia Jennings), she suddenly opens up her blouse and asks, "Do these look like the boobs of a 40-year-old woman?" Friday answers in his usual serious voice, "Excellent, bordering on spectacular."

DRAGNET, 1987

425 Murderers come with smiles

This American gangster movie reminds you of your mother's warnings not to play with the bad boys, especially in the classic bar scene, in which psychotic killer Joe Pesci turns on wannabe-gangster Ray Liotta for apparently laughing at him: "Funny how? I mean, funny like I'm a clown? I amuse you? I make you laugh?"

GOODFELLAS, 1990

426 "I don't know nuthin', I don't see nuthin', I don't hear nuthin'"

Gangster Tony Camonte denies having anything to do with the murder of his boss, Louis Costillo, when questioned by police. He even has an alibi: "I was having my beauty sleep—in the lady's house."

SCARFACE: THE SHAME OF A NATION, 1932

427 A cast as explosive as its story!

As a powerful hurricane sweeps over the Florida Keys, war veteran Frank McCloud stands up to gangster Johnny Rocco, who is starting to show signs of strain: "You don't like it, do you Rocco, the storm? Show it your gun, why don't you? If it doesn't stop, shoot it."

KEY LARGO, 1948

428 Hired killers by day Devoted lovers by night

The most shocking moment in this movie comes when Mafia hit man Charley Partanna ceases his indecision—"Do I ice her? Do I marry her?"—and settles the score with his hit-woman lover, Irene Walker…

PRIZZI'S HONOR, 1985

429 Doyle is bad news—but a good cop

In a great opening scene, NYPD cop Jimmy "Popeye" Doyle, dressed as Santa Claus, and his partner Buddy Russo, dressed as a hot dog vendor, pursue a suspect through Brooklyn.

THE FRENCH CONNECTION, 1971

430 "I'm Winston Wolf. I solve problems."

This movie has many memorable scenes, but one fantastically absurd moment is when Wolf—"the cleaner"—gets Vincent and Jules to pick up little pieces of brain and skull from the interior of their blood-drenched Chevy Nova before Jimmie's wife comes home and finds a dead body in her garage!

PULP FICTION, 1994

431 You don't assign him to murder cases...You just turn him loose.

In a much-repeated, but utterly unforgettable scene, Clint Eastwood coolly aims his gun at a bank robber: "I know what you're thinking. Did he fire six shots, or only five? Well, to tell you the truth, in all this excitement, I've kinda lost track myself. But being as this is a .44 Magnum, the most powerful handgun in the world, and would blow your head clean off, you've got to ask yourself one question: Do I feel lucky? Well, do ya, punk?"

DIRTY HARRY, 1971

432 Never give Candy to strangers...

John Candy tries to prove his innocence by retracing the route a murderer probably took from his hotel room, down a ladder, across a narrow beam to a balcony, through a set of French doors, and into a room—then the lights are clicked on. He is at the scene of the crime and is now the prime suspect!

ONCE UPON A CRIME, 1992

433 Caught short!

Ray Barboni is in the bathroom, reading a book while sitting on the toilet, when the phone rings—it's great to be reminded that even gangsters have ordinary problems!

GET SHORTY, 1995

434 The rhythm method!

While Dorothy dances with her fiancé, the suave former-detective Nick Charles illustrates the art of mixing martinis to the bartenders: "The important thing is the rhythm! Always have rhythm in your shaking. Now, a Manhattan, you shake to fox-trot time, a Bronx, to two-step time, a dry martini, you always shake to waltz time."

THE THIN MAN, 1934

435 It will mark you for life as it marked him for... betrayal

Insane killer Tommy Udo ties an old woman to a wheelchair and laughs sadistically as he pushes her down a long flight of stairs...
KISS OF DEATH, 1947

436 Don't get him all steamed up

Gangster Cody Jarrett leaps from the ledge of a tunnel's mouth and makes his way toward the front of the train:
Engineer: "What's this, a hold-up?"
Jarrett: "Naw, naw, you're seven minutes late. We're just changin' engineers."
WHITE HEAT, 1949

437 It's *The Godfather* on laughing gas

Connie Russo points a gun at Tony Russo's "family jewels" and he desperately covers his crotch with his hands. She shoots. He suddenly wakes up, startled, in a prison cell—it seems it was all just a strange dream...
MARRIED TO THE MOB, 1988

438 America's most infamous criminals!

When Clyde discovers that the bank has collapsed and has no money for him to steal, he asks the teller to explain it to Bonnie. She laughs at the absurd situation, and Clyde shoots out the bank's window in frustration: "We got a dollar ninety-eight and you're laughing!"

BONNIE AND CLYDE, 1967

439 Tough and brutal

Walker wants revenge. He bursts into a room and empties his gun into an empty bed...his wife's bed...the bed in which she cheated on him with his best friend...who shot him and left him for dead...

POINT BLANK, 1967

440 Eliot Ness and a small force of men swore they'd bring him down

Frank Nitti makes a wrong move when he provokes Federal Agent Eliot Ness by saying, "Your friend died screaming like a stuck Irish pig." Ness furiously grabs Nitti and throws him off the building ledge. Nitti shrieks as he falls, and Ness calls after him, "Did it sound anything like that?"

THE UNTOUCHABLES, 1987

441

A perfect assassin. An innocent girl. They have nothing left to lose except each other.

After the intense time she spent with professional hit man Léon, the little girl Mathilda seeks sanctuary at an orphanage: "OK. My family, they got shot down by DEA officers because of a drug problem. I left with the greatest guy on Earth. He was a hit man, the best in town, but he died this morning. And if you don't help me, I'll be dead by tonight."

LÉON, 1994

442

"It's not faith, it's work."

In a chilling death scene, convicted murderer Matthew Poncelet is strapped into the apparatus, ready for his lethal injection in the death chamber. Sister Helen Prejean tells him, "I want the last face you see in this world to be the face of love, so you look at me when they do this thing. I'll be the face of love for you."

DEAD MAN WALKING, 1995

443 A rum case

Private Investigator Marlowe is hired by General Sternwood to find his aide, Sean Regan, who has disappeared—something it seems the gumshoe has done before:

Sternwood: "You knew him, too?"

Marlowe: "Yes, in the old days, when he used to run rum out of Mexico, and I was on the other side. We used to swap shots between drinks, or drinks between shots, whichever you like."

THE BIG SLEEP, 1946

444 Every dog had his day

Mr. White and Mr. Pink make their view of the police perfectly clear as they try to figure out how the robbery went sour:

Mr. Pink: "You kill anybody?"

Mr. White: "A few cops."

Mr. Pink: "No real people?"

Mr. White: "Just cops."

RESERVOIR DOGS, 1992

445 Should have called a locksmith

The only evidence that can implicate Ray Milland in a murder is a door key. The tension mounts as he becomes confused over the comings and goings of the various keys, and it reaches the boiling point when he opens the door with the one key that will prove his guilt!

DIAL M FOR MURDER, 1954

446 It came as quite a blow

Iris Henderson befriends Miss Froy, a kind old woman, on the train, but when someone suddenly knocks Iris out, Miss Froy vanishes—and is replaced by someone else who is wearing the old woman's clothes.

THE LADY VANISHES, 1938

447 The men who broke the bank—and lost the cargo!

Shy and retiring Mr. Holland, who has been a faithful bank employee for 20 years, waits patiently while his partner smelts down the gold they have stolen and reshapes it into souvenir Eiffel Towers, so he can smuggle it out of the country.

THE LAVENDER HILL MOB, 1951

448 You don't crucify people! Not on Good Friday!

This is one of those great British gangster movies that sets your nerves on edge and leaves them there. Bob Hoskins is kidnapped outside London's Savoy Hotel by the gangsters he'd crossed earlier. As he is driven away, he realizes that it's curtains for him!
THE LONG GOOD FRIDAY, 1980

449 Anyone for grapefruit?

Tom is growing tired of his girlfriend Kitty. When she suggests that he shouldn't have alcohol before breakfast, he impulsively grabs a grapefruit half from the table and pushes it into her face.
THE PUBLIC ENEMY, 1931

450 If the shoe fits

Wealthy executive Gondo mortgages his property to raise the money to take over a famous shoe empire. The night before the deal, he receives a telephone call from kidnappers, who demand a huge ransom for the return of his son. But the boy they've got isn't his— they have mistakenly taken his chauffeur's son. Gondo is faced with the dilemma of becoming financially or morally bankrupt.
HIGH AND LOW, 1963

Drama

Drama is one of the most wide-ranging of genres, and more movies probably fit into this category than into any other. We turn to these movies when we want a more realistic view of life, because they portray "real" people in real-life situations. Dramas are often serious movies that deal with the important issues of the times, but they may also be lighthearted, exciting, romantic, melodramatic, or harrowing, and they sometimes deal with factual events and famous historical figures.

Previous page: Sue Lyon in *Lolita* (1962).

451 A story of the most precious moments in a woman's life!

An express train flies past a railway station, throwing a piece of grit into a woman's eye. By pure chance, a handsome doctor is there to help. It's the beginning of a beautiful relationship that is destined not to last.

BRIEF ENCOUNTER, 1945

452 "I am a human being!"

John Merrick escapes the freak show and the brutish handling of his keeper, Bytes. With sackcloth covering his head and face, he tries to make his way back to London. At the train station, he attracts a rowdy crowd, who unhood him, to their horror. Merrick musters all his courage and humanity, and proclaims: "I am not an animal!"

THE ELEPHANT MAN, 1980

453 "I must be crazy to be in a loony bin like this!"

In an American insane asylum, one patient is a well-built Indian man who convinces everyone that he is mute—until fellow inmate, Jack Nicholson, offers him a stick of gum, at which he sighs appreciatively, "Mmmm, Juicy Fruit."

ONE FLEW OVER THE CUCKOO'S NEST, 1975

454 Garbo talks!

Anna Christie (Greta Garbo), seeking redemption from her estranged father, makes her grand entrance into a waterfront saloon from a foggy street. She sits across from her father's boozing companion, Marthy (Marie Dressler), and speaks in her deep husky voice, "Give me a whisky, ginger ale on the side, and don't be stingy, baby."

ANNA CHRISTIE, 1930

455 She's married two years—quite a girl—and not quite a woman

Archie Lee peers lecherously through a small hole in the wall at his luscious blonde 19-year-old wife, who is lying on a crib, sucking her thumb. She hears him trying to make the hole bigger, gets up, and comes into his room: "Archie Lee! You're a mess. Do you know what they call such people? Peepin' Toms!"

BABY DOLL, 1956

456 Of all the girls in the world, he had to pick her.

At an outdoor swimming pool, young Jake la Motta becomes lustfully attracted to a fifteen-year-old blonde named Vickie, who hangs around with the wiseguys. He becomes obsessed with her, and incessantly grills his brother about her: "Where's she from? What's her last name? She knows them? She go with them?..."

RAGING BULL, 1980

457 New mother

There's a short, but memorable, scene before the opening credits that shows Shirley MacLaine as a worried new mother checking on her baby every five minutes through the night. She imagines the worst as she stares at the crib of her infant daughter: "Rudyard, she's not breathing!" She shakes the baby out of its peaceful sleep, causing it to wail. "That's better."

TERMS OF ENDEARMENT, 1983

458 "I'll tell you one thing, I don't ever want to be like him."

Jim Stark (James Dean) wishes his father would stop being a henpecked, ineffectual "chicken" and stand up to his domineering wife, who is only concerned about keeping up an image of respectability: "if he had guts to knock Mom cold once, then maybe she'd be happy, and then she'd stop pickin' on him because they make mush out of him."

REBEL WITHOUT A CAUSE, 1955

459 In 1959 a lot of people were killing time. Kit and Holly were killing people.

Kit stands at the edge of the river and points to an uprooted tree which is now just driftwood laying in the water. "The river must've washed the roots away," suggests Holly. Kit finds a heavy stone and suggests they use it to crunch their hands to commemorate their first sexual union, but Holly objects.

BADLANDS, 1973

460 A bird in the hand...

John McTeague works in a mine by candlelight. He inspects a chunk of rock quartz and throws it into the pile with the rest. As he pushes a rail-car out of the mouth of the tunnel, he spots a little lame bird on the ground in the middle of the track, picks it up, and gently kisses it.

GREED, 1925

461 The fine art of social interaction

Private Maggio and the bullying, sadistic Sergeant "Fatso" Judson get into a fight when Maggio criticizes Fatso's piano playing.

Fatso: "I'll play loud as I want, you little Wap."

Maggio: "Little Wap!? Mess with me, fat stuff, and I'll bust ya up."

FROM HERE TO ETERNITY, 1953

462 "That's our man—he's made-to-order."

After publishing a fictitious letter by a supposedly suicidal man against an unjust political system, the newspaper must find someone to pose as the author. They eventually discover a plain-speaking, homeless, ex-baseball player named "Long John" Willoughby, who almost collapses into a chair at the first sight of food.

MEET JOHN DOE, 1941

463 In the spirit of democracy

Hungover politician Willie Stark lurches onto the stage to give a speech at a campaign barbecue.

Sadie: "How'd you get him here? He was out stiff."

Jack: "The hair of the dog that bit him."

Sadie: "Hair? He must have swallowed the dog."

ALL THE KING'S MEN, 1949

464 "There's a lot of ugly things in this world, son."

Farmer Cunningham drives up in his horse-drawn wagon and, with some embarrassment, delivers a sack of nuts to the Finch residence, as partial payment for some legal work. One of the Finch children asks his lawyer father about the man:

Scout: "Is he poor?"

Atticus: "Yes."

Scout: "Are we poor?"

Atticus: "We are indeed."

Scout: "Are we as poor as the Cunninghams?"

Atticus: "No, not exactly…"

TO KILL A MOCKINGBIRD, 1962

465 Street crimes

The Prince of Verona scolds the youths of two households for disturbing the peace of the town three times. The penalty for further fights and violations of the peace, he says, shall be death: "If you ever disturb our streets again, your lives shall pay the forfeit of the peace. For this time all the rest depart away. You, Capulet, shall go along with me. And Montague, come you this afternoon. Once more, on pain of death, all men depart."

ROMEO AND JULIET, 1968

466 Fear can hold you prisoner. Hope can set you free.

Inmate Andy Dufresne discovers a set of records. He places one on the record player in the office, locks the doors, and broadcasts Mozart's *The Marriage of Figaro* throughout the entire prison. "It was like some beautiful bird flapped into our drab little cage and made those walls dissolve away. And for the briefest of moments, every last man at Shawshank felt free."

THE SHAWSHANK REDEMPTION, 1994

467 An improvised moment

Terry Malloy and Edie Doyle walk together through a playground; he is trying to be friendly, but she remains distant. She tells him that she went to school in the country, and Terry replies, "I don't like the country, the crickets make me nervous." Edie drops her white glove, and Terry picks it up and tries it on his own hand.

ON THE WATERFRONT, 1954

468 The South's greatest romance

When Preston arrives to accompany Julie to a society ball, he is shocked to find her dressed in a flaming red, bare-shouldered dress. She challenges her beau to escort her.

Julie: "Well, shall we go, Pres?"

Preston: "Not 'til you're properly dressed."

Julie: "You're sure it's the dress? It couldn't be that you're afraid, afraid somebody'd insult me and you'd find it necessary to defend me."

JEZEBEL, 1938

469 "Uh, well, sir, I ain't a fer-real cowboy. But I am one helluva stud!"

Joe drags Ratso onto a bus bound for Florida so his friend can realize his dreams, and Ratso wants to make some changes: "I hope we're not gonna have a lot of trouble about my name down there. Can you see this guy runnin' around the beach all sun-tanned, and he's goin' in swimmin' like, and somebody yells, 'Hey, Ratso!' I'm Rico all the time, OK?"

MIDNIGHT COWBOY, 1969

470 Strange drama of a captive sweetheart!

Gregory walks away into the foggy night, but stops just around the corner, taking care to keep out of sight. Shortly afterward, the gaslights flicker and dim. In the house, his wife hears ominous footsteps above her, which she believes are in her mind. But Gregory is up in the attic trying to locate the precious jewels he thinks are hidden among her aunt's possessions.

GASLIGHT, 1944

225

471 It was a time that changed the world. And one man put it to music.

Miller is conducting his big band at an open-air concert for injured servicemen when a German V1 flying bomb appears overhead. Its engine suddenly cuts and the spectators run for cover, but the band magnificently keeps playing "In the Mood." The bomb explodes nearby and the band triumphantly strikes up the final crescendo, to the cheers of the crowd.

THE GLEN MILLER STORY, 1953

472 One of the great ones!

White convict Johnny "Joker" Jackson and black convict Noah Cullen try to jump a freight train to freedom. Cullen gets on and locks hands with his companion but can't pull him aboard. He sacrifices his own freedom and falls onto the ground. In their final few moments, they share a cigarette, and Cullen sings the blues classic "Long Gone" as the bloodhounds close in on them.

THE DEFIANT ONES, 1958

473 "The list is life."

Accountant Itzhak Stern types quickly as he and Oskar Schindler struggle hard to remember…to remember names—as many names as possible, for each name represents a life…a Jewish life that will only be saved if it appears on that list as an employee of the factory.

SCHINDLER'S LIST, 1993

474 Things look different the closer you get

The sequence of the photographer obsessively processing and blowing up the pictures he took in the park is the most memorable moment in this movie. He magnifies the photos again and again, until they finally reveal a man, a gun, and what could be a dead body…

BLOW-UP, 1966

475 Ungentlemanly conduct

Mario and Jo are transporting explosives across hostile terrain. Jo panics, fearing they will plunge into a ravine, and refuses to go any further. There is a standoff between the two men—Mario has a rock, Joe has a heavy branch. Mario orders Jo to drop his weapon, then throws the rock at the other man's head and kicks him in the groin.

THE WAGES OF FEAR, 1953

476 This, in its own terrifying way, is a love story.

Drunk Joe Clay forces his alcoholic wife to take a good look in the mirror: "I walked by the Union Square Bar. I was going to go in. Then I saw myself—my reflection in the window—and I thought, 'I wonder who that bum is.' And then I saw it was me. Now look at me. I'm a bum. Look at me. Look at you. You're a bum. Look at you. And look at us. Look at us. C'mon, look at us. See? A couple of bums."

DAYS OF WINE AND ROSES, 1962

477 A story that really boils over!

Local girl Kathie discovers that the motorcycle gang that has brought fear to her small town is called the Black Rebels. She asks the leather-clad leader, "What are you rebelling against?" To which Johnny magnificently replies, "Waddya got?"

THE WILD ONE, 1953

478 Based on a true story

Two big-game hunters spend an evening under the spell of Karen Blixen. At her request, Denys makes up the first line of a story, which she then completes—holding them both enthralled for hours.

OUT OF AFRICA, 1985

479 On the chain gang, they'd seen every kind of man—but Luke became a legend.

Penitentiary life in the Deep South is momentarily lightened when legendary convict Luke accepts a bet to eat fifty hardboiled eggs in one hour!

COOL HAND LUKE, 1967

480 It takes two to tango

Blind retired army officer Frank Slade enjoys one final fling in New York. In a plush restaurant, he is drawn to a beautiful young woman by only her scent. He convinces her to dance with him, and they light up the screen with one of the sexiest tangos ever filmed.

SCENT OF A WOMAN, 1992

481 Everybody sings in Wales

Paul Robeson plays a black Pennsylvanian working in a South Wales coal mine who is accepted by the other miners when they realize that they all look the same when covered in coal dust. Robeson holds them—and us—spellbound with his singing voice when he competes with the choir at the Eisteddfod.

PROUD VALLEY, 1940

482 How did they ever make a movie of *Lolita*?

In an attempt to convince Professor Humbert to be her lodger, Charlotte shows him her garden: "My flowers win prizes around here! They're the talk of the neighborhood. Voilà!" It's our first view of her nubile twelve-year-old daughter, Dolores "Lolita" Haze, languidly sunbathing on a blanket on the lawn. Lolita looks up and throws an expressionless stare at Humbert.

LOLITA, 1962

483 It's the love story of an unsung hero!

Herb offers Marty five bucks to take his date off his hands: "I got stuck on a blind date with a dog. And I just met an old girl I used to know. I was wondering how I'm gonna get rid of the girl I'm with. Somebody to take her home." Marty nobly refuses: "You can't just walk off on a girl like that." He then watches as another man is offered the same deal.

MARTY, 1955

484 If you're an Eastman, you're not in the same boat with anyone.

Earl Eastman gives his cousin, George, a tour of the family factory and warns him about keeping the great family name unsullied: "There's a company rule against any of us mixing socially with the girls who work here. My father asked me to particularly call this to your attention. That is a must."

A PLACE IN THE SUN, 1951

485 A film for all time

Sir Thomas More is on trial in this epic movie, and we must watch an innocent man being given no chance whatsoever to defend himself.

A MAN FOR ALL SEASONS, 1966

486 From minor to major

Tyrone Power plays the famous concert pianist Eddy Duchin, who was diagnosed with an incurable disease, in this true story. In one poignant scene, he is playing beautifully on a grand piano when his little boy joins in on another piano, to startling effect.

THE EDDY DUCHIN STORY, 1956

487 Homeward bound

Three war veterans share the cramped space in the observation cone of an airforce bomber as it flies low across America. They share one common bond—the same hometown—and they marvel at the landscape below:

Homer: "Boy oh boy, hey, look at that. Look at those automobiles down there. You can see them so plain, you can even see the people in them."

Fred: "Yeah, it looks like we're flying by a roadmap."

THE BEST YEARS OF OUR LIVES, 1946

488 Television will never be the same!

Veteran news anchor Howard Beale learns that he's being let go. He tells viewers that he's going to kill himself during his final broadcast, and the viewing figures go through the roof. He urges his viewers, "I want all of you to get up out of your chairs. I want you to get up right now and go to the window. Open it, and stick your head out, and yell, 'I'm as mad as hell, and I'm not going to take it anymore!'"

NETWORK, 1976

489 This is the story of J. J. But not the way he wants it told!

Desperate agent Sidney phones angered columnist J. J. Hunsecker to ask him to come out of the Twenty One Club so that the two can talk in private:

Hunsecker: "You had to do something for me—you didn't do it."

Sidney: "Could I come in for a minute?"

Hunsecker: "No. You're dead, son. Get yourself buried."

SWEET SMELL OF SUCCESS, 1957

490 There is a miracle in being young... and a fear...

A teenage boy and girl are sitting in an open, yellow roadster convertible on lover's lane. They are passionately kissing and breathing heavily as the water churns over the waterfall behind them. Bud pleads with his sweetheart to go further:

Bud: "Deanie, please..."

Deanie: "Bud, I'm afraid. Don't, Bud."

Bud: "Deanie..."

SPLENDOR IN THE GRASS, 1961

233

491 The sweet life

Nana is a lost and desperate young woman who is drawn to a life of acting, then turns to prostitution in her quest to live *la dolce vita*. In one brief, mesmerizing scene, the camera follows effortlessly as she dances joyfully and uninhibitedly around a billiards room.

MY LIFE TO LIVE, 1962

492 Happy anniversary!

As soon as Charlene's boyfriend arrives, the couple retreat to the back row of the picture house. She gets rid of her chewing gum and they start kissing. Sonny peers at the face of the young star on the big screen and wishes he were kissing her instead.

THE LAST PICTURE SHOW, 1971

493 Diary of a dipsomaniac

Don Birman eloquently describes the empowering benefits of booze: "It tosses the sandbags overboard so the balloon can soar. Suddenly, I'm above the ordinary. I'm competent…I'm walking a tightrope over Niagara Falls. I'm one of the great ones. I'm Michelangelo, molding the beard of Moses. I'm Van Gogh, painting pure sunlight…"

THE LOST WEEKEND, 1945

494 They called him "Fast Eddie"

Paul Newman downs bourbon while playing pool in a bar. He feigns drunkenness and makes bad shots to entice the other players into betting against him. He then makes an almost impossible shot. Someone says, "you couldn't make that shot again in a million years." He repeats the shot, with higher stakes, and misses. The bartender and patrons challenge the pool player to another attempt and match his bet—"one week's commission," or $105. They are being hustled.
THE HUSTLER, 1961

495 This is war! This is not a game of cricket!

The Japanese colonel of a prisoner-of-war camp emerges from his hut to greet his newly arrived British prisoners: "I am Colonel Saito. You British prisoners have been chosen to build a bridge across the River Kwai. Escape is impossible. Today you rest. Tomorrow you begin. Let me remind you of the General's motto: 'Be happy in your work.' Dismissed."
THE BRIDGE ON THE RIVER KWAI, 1957

496 Dying to know you...

Tom Joad is hitchhiking home to his family's farm after serving a short prison term. The truck driver studies him suspiciously, so Tom satisfies his curiosity: "You're about to bust a gut to know what I done, ain't ya? Well, I ain't a guy to let ya down. Homicide!"

THE GRAPES OF WRATH, 1940

497 There's no such thing as a free lunch!

Veteran James Allen returns from the war to a life on the streets. A fellow drifter named Pete proposes going to a lunch wagon that hands out hamburgers. Hungry and destitute, Allen responds, "What would I say to a hamburger? Oh, boy. I'd shake Mr. Hamburger by the hand and say, 'Pal, I haven't seen you in a long, long time.'"

I AM A FUGITIVE FROM A CHAIN GANG, 1932

498 In the shadow of the gallows

Orson Welles makes a spellbinding and impassioned speech against the death penalty as a defense attorney representing two college students on trial for murdering a young boy.

COMPULSION, 1959

499 "I move around a lot."

Jack Nicholson makes a painful confession to his dying father in the cold outdoors. He apologizes for abandoning his family and his talent, and for not living up to his father's ideals: "Not because I'm looking for anything, really. But—'cause I'm getting away from things that get bad if I stay. The best that I can do is apologize. I'm sorry it didn't work out."

FIVE EASY PIECES, 1970

500 Suddenly, last summer, Cathy knew she was being used for something evil!

Catherine describes the murder of her homosexual cousin Sebastian, and how he had used her to attract and lure boys while they were traveling together in Spain: "He—he was lying naked on the broken stones—and this you won't believe! Nobody, nobody, nobody could believe it! It looked as if—as if they had devoured him! As if they'd torn or cut parts of him away with their hands, or with knives, or those jagged tin cans they made music with. As if they'd torn bits of him away in strips!"

SUDDENLY, LAST SUMMER, 1959

B Movies

B movies are almost impossible to define, but we all know them when we see them! The term was originally given to the low-budget productions of the 1930s that were created to support the A movies. Somehow the term "B movie" quickly became pejorative, but many classic B movies have attracted a cult following. There is something about the complete lack of sophistication and low-rate special effects that people love—it's great fun to see the strings on the flying saucers and the man's feet sticking out of the bottom of the awful monster suit—and we can all laugh at the cheesy dialogue, bad acting, and predictable plots. Still, B movies have an indisputable charm that makes them oddly appealing—and impossible to forget.

Previous page: Joan Taylor and Hugh Marlowe in
Earth vs. the Flying Saucers (1956).

501 "Hey, can somebody please pass the ketchup?"

A housewife washing dishes stares in disbelief as a ripe, red tomato emerges from her garbage disposal. Her disbelief turns to sheer terror as the ferocious fruit launches a savage attack upon her!

ATTACK OF THE KILLER TOMATOES, 1978

502 Bogged down!

In a foggy Texas swamp, mad scientist Dr. Simond Trent leans over a glass tank in his laboratory and speaks to the strange creature inside it: "You're ready. Awake! The sound of my voice is your master! Get up! Get up! The world awaits you as my first citizen!"

CURSE OF THE SWAMP CREATURE, 1966

503 Flying beast out of prehistoric skies!

A team investigating rumors of a UFO flies out to the site of an aircraft crash. Suddenly a "bird as big as a battleship" attacks their plane. The men bail out as their plane is destroyed, but they aren't safe yet—the bird circles back and gobbles up the parachutists one by one.

THE GIANT CLAW, 1957

504 You can't scream if you can't breathe

Snake expert Paul Sarone finds and
unravels a thirty-five-foot-long snake skin:
Danny: "What's this?"
Paul: "Anaconda skin."
Danny: "There's snakes out there this big?!"
Paul: "This skin is three or four years old. Whatever
shed it has grown since then..."
ANACONDA, 1997

505 New thrills! New shocks! New terror!

A reporter and a military colonel discover that a small town was
completely destroyed by giant grasshoppers. When they question
scientist Ed Wainwright, who is running an agricultural research
project nearby, they realize that he might have had something to do
with it: "Are you trying to tell me you bred these things!?"

BEGINNING OF THE END, 1957

506 A bad case of wind

The evil magician Alquazar (Christopher Lee), watching through his magic mirror, casts a spell that sends a cyclic wind tearing through his city to catch the rebels that are plotting to overthrow him.

ARABIAN ADVENTURE, 1979

507 The day the earth split in two!

A scientist experimenting with geothermal energy causes a huge and deadly crack to appear in the earth's crust. Dr. Ted Rampion has to explain the implications to the politicians, "Where the land masses split, the oceans will be sucked in, and the colossal pressure generated by the steam will rip the earth apart—and destroy it!"

CRACK IN THE WORLD, 1965

508 Your worst fears can come true

A deputy sheriff stops to investigate a suspicious car parked outside an abandoned farmhouse. He climbs up to take a look through a hole in the wall and sees a group of travelers inside. They ignore his calls. Suddenly, out of the darkness, something launches itself at him...

DEADLY INVASION: THE KILLER BEE NIGHTMARE, 1995

509 Love-starved moon maidens on the prowl!

Five astronauts discover a huge modern city on the dark side of the moon and are given a warm welcome by the last surviving members of an ancient civilization. In one scene, the lovely leotard-clad ladies perform a seductive dance for the astronauts, and once the men fall under their power, they plan to steal their spaceship.

CAT-WOMEN OF THE MOON, 1953

510 Home movies

Jazz musician Fred Madison is unhappily married to Renee, whom he suspects of infidelity. The couple start finding anonymous videotapes outside their home. The first shows only the front of the house, but the second was shot inside and shows them asleep in their bedroom. The couple calls the police, who do nothing to help, but then Fred finds another tape, which shows him killing his wife.

LOST HIGHWAY, 1997

511 The whole world is under attack!

A flying saucer lands at the Skyhook control center during a rocket launch, and three aliens emerge. The military shoot one of them, and the aliens retaliate by destroying the Skyhook center. They give the humans a cryptic warning and tell them to "arrange for your world leaders to confer with us in the city of Washington, D.C."

EARTH VS. THE FLYING SAUCERS, 1956

512 "I knew I was up against something strange, but a 500-pound bloodsucking beanbag?!"

A murder investigation takes a strange turn when private eye Dick Trent is told that the victims' bodies contain traces of an alien presence. "Whatever it is, it shouldn't be there, because it's not human, that's what it's not!"

THE ROLY POLY MAN, 1994

513 Double the terror, double the fun.

A young boy becomes traumatized after being caught watching a couple having sex. The man beats him severely while the woman laughs at him—it's bound to have an effect on him!

EDGE OF SANITY, 1989

514 "Welcome..."

Jonathan Harker is picked up on a dark, foggy road by a mysterious coachman, and he is chased by howling wolves as he travels to the castle. Once he's inside, the enigmatic Count Dracula shows him to his room and Harker is startled to see that the Count casts no reflection in a mirror.

COUNT DRACULA, 1970

515 Out with the old

In the opening scene, an unconscious man is carried to Queen Omphale of Lydia on a stretcher. As she caresses this new arrival, Omphale gestures to her guards, who draw their swords and kill her old lover...

HERCULES UNCHAINED, 1959

516 Suddenly he could see through clothes, flesh...and walls!

When his funding is cut, Dr. James Xavier decides to test his new drug on himself. With the help of a reluctant colleague, he drops the liquid into his eyes. First, he sees only a brilliant light, but soon he finds that he can see through surfaces, read papers in closed folders, see a pen in someone's pocket...

X: THE MAN WITH THE X-RAY EYES, 1963

517 A baboon that plays chess!

One of Sinbad's sailors is amazed when he enters Princess Farah's cabin and sees her playing chess with a baboon. A distraught Farah begs him to leave, but Sinbad has to step in and explain the truth: "He is not really a baboon. He was transformed by the black arts of Queen Zenobia's witchcraft. He is Prince Kassim..."

SINBAD AND THE EYE OF THE TIGER, 1977

518 There's no place on Earth to hide!

A meteor capable of destroying mankind is heading for Earth and scientific advisor Harry Sherwood (Karl Madden) has to convince Dr. Paul Bradley (Sean Connery, in a role he'd probably rather forget!) to lead a mission to destroy it. Feeling that he's heard enough, Connery magnificently says, "Why don't you stick a broom up my ass? That way I can sweep the floor on my way out."

METEOR, 1979

519 Rootin' tootin' stuff

As "acting sheriff," Slim's first duty is to sweep the sheriff's office. He stops in front of a "wanted" poster of Adolf Hitler, draws his unloaded gun, points it at the picture, and squeezes off two clicks. Then he sits down and plays the broom like a guitar, while singing, "I'm gonna get der Führer, sure as shootin'…"

COWBOY COMMANDOS, 1943

520 The green slime is coming!

Astronauts sent to blow up a huge asteroid called Flora, which is on a collision course with Earth, get more than they bargained for when scientist Dr. Halverson runs over to them, excitedly shouts, "It's alive!" and shows them a jar filled with green goo.

THE GREEN SLIME, 1968

521 It is coming

As a small seaside town prepares to celebrate its centennial, an old sailor sits on the beach, telling a group of enthralled children a ghostly tale. One hundred years earlier, a ship full of lepers was destroyed on the rocks when it followed a signal fire that had been intentionally lit by a group of the town's first settlers.

THE FOG, 1980

522 Nothing human loves forever

When Catherine Deneuve's lover (David Bowie) becomes old, frail, and repulsive, the 2000-year-old vampire locks him in a coffin and leaves him to rot forgotten in her attic...surrounded by similar boxes.

THE HUNGER, 1983

523 Every man its prisoner... every woman its slave

Mankind's first satellite is being brought back to Earth by a team of scientists. They lose control of it, and the satellite crashes into the mountains. As the camera surveys the ruins shortly afterward, we clearly see something freeing itself from the wreckage…

IT CONQUERED THE WORLD, 1956

524 Drug-crazed abandon!

Crusading high-school principal Dr. Carroll explains at a student's trial how he easily diagnosed Bill's marijuana habit: Bill showed signs of "disassociation of ideas" and even "missed the ball by three or four feet" while playing tennis.

TELL YOUR CHILDREN, 1938

525 The Devil exists, and the Eye knows where.

A statue with a single, glowing red eye stands in a jewelry shop in Chinatown. Three masked ninjas enter, kill the shop owner, and attempt to pry the eye from the statue. Then the police arrive and a vicious fight begins…

THE LOST EMPIRE, 1983

526 The first citizen of the underwater republic

A team of divers comes upon a mysterious sea creature with fins, silvery skin, and large eyes. The locals dub it "the sea devil." In one beautifully shot underwater scene, the sea creature, Ichthyander, dreams of himself and the attractive young girl he has fallen in love with, living and swimming together under the sea.

AMPHIBIAN MAN, 1961

527 Sharp-fanged blood-sucking death dives from midnight skies!

Dr. Paul Carruthers (Bela Lugosi) hides a deadly secret in the attic above his laboratory—a giant bat that he created by exposing a normal bat to electrical impulses! One night, he angers the creature by waving a scent under its nose. He then releases it into the village...

THE DEVIL BAT, 1940

528 "It's all over now, isn't it?"

Australia is the only country not yet affected by a devastating nuclear holocaust, and the survivors can only wait for the deadly radiation that is on its way to their shores. Then they receive a radio signal coming from America, where they thought no life remained...

ON THE BEACH, 1959

529 When the screen screams you'll scream too...if you value your life!

This film opens with its director, William Castle, telling the audience that, for the first time in movie history, they will feel "some of the physical reactions" that the characters feel on screen. He adds that only people sensitive to "mysterious electronic impulses" will feel this "tingling sensation," but they can defend themselves by screaming!

THE TINGLER, 1959

530 "I have a gift for disaster."

John Morlar is watching television when someone enters his apartment and savagely hits him with a small statuette, leaving him dead. The following morning, as the police inspect his body, Morlar suddenly starts breathing again!

THE MEDUSA TOUCH, 1978

531 Dream girl

Glen is preparing to tell his fiancée, Barbara, that he is a transvestite, and his mind is running riot: he imagines himself dressed as his alter ego, Glenda, surrounded by disapproving people and wrestling with Barbara. Bela Lugosi appears, followed by a troupe of strippers, and then the Devil, who volunteers to be best man at his wedding.

GLEN OR GLENDA, 1953

532 A damp start

Outside it is raining, and inside we see a puff of smoke in the darkness. Alain Delon gets out of bed, puts on a trench coat and hat, and leaves the room. He climbs into an unlocked car and tries several of a large set of keys—the tools of his trade—until the engine starts, allowing him to speed away to his lover to arrange his alibi.

THE GODSON, 1967

533 The most colossal conflict the screen has ever known!

A U.S. submarine collides with a strange iceberg that is beginning to melt in the Bering Strait. Helicopter pilots come to rescue the crew, and they suddenly spot a huge creature in the water. Godzilla has been released from his icy prison—and he is heading for Japan!

KING KONG VS. GODZILLA, 1962

534 They prey on human flesh!

A Brazilian man and his son break into a research station to steal experimental bees that they think will produce more honey. But the bees are a new aggressive strain of killer bees, and they sting the two men to death.

THE BEES, 1978

535 Hypnotized! Reincarnated as a monster from hell!

A mysterious mesmerizer returns his beautiful assistant to a previous life, and she climbs out of the water as a hideous monster covered in scales, claws, and tusks. "Now, on this very night, I have called her from the unknown depths of time itself! She is here...the world will never again be as it was!"

THE SHE-CREATURE, 1956

536 Christmas comes but once a year

The movie opens on a street corner at night. A man in a Santa suit is standing there. The camera follows him as he gets into a car with a girl. Santa looks straight at the camera and says, "Go on! Go away! Clear off!" He then gets out of the car and is stabbed in the stomach with a long knife. The girl backs away, but is stabbed, too...Then the music starts up: "Jingle bells..."

DON'T OPEN 'TIL CHRISTMAS, 1984

537 From the caverns of the deep…it strikes!

An apologetic scientist explains to a scared community just what is attacking them: "They took five death-row inmates and injected them with a genetic code of sorts, taken from different species of fish…" But one incredulous listener is much more succinct: "Fishmen!"

HUMANOIDS FROM THE DEEP, 1996

538 "I, Proteus…"

A mobile robotic arm carries Susan Harris to a laboratory. She awakes to find herself strapped to a bed and undergoing a complete physiological examination—by the computer Proteus! "I, Proteus, possess the wisdom and ignorance of all men—but I can't feel the sun on my face. My child will have that privilege."

DEMON SEED, 1977

539 "The alien enemy is trying to destroy us with our stupidity and our weaknesses!"

Astronauts on the planet Uranus discover a bizarre fantasy world that contains places and people from their childhoods. They eventually make their way through the force field imprisoning them and come face-to-face with their enemy—a giant, pulsating brain!

JOURNEY TO THE SEVENTH PLANET, 1962

540 "They breed, you know..."

In the opening scene, a truck heading for the San Diego Zoo is carrying cargo marked, "Venomous Reptile—Handle with Extreme Care." The truck crashes into a tree. As the passenger pulls himself free, he hears an agonized scream from the driver. He returns to the truck to find the driver dead. Then he spots a huge rattlesnake...

SILENT PREDATORS, 1999

541 "You know, honey, what you need is a nice, long vacation..."

Dr. Lester Cavigny watches in horror as his daughter sleepwalks into his study, takes a gun from his drawer, and returns to bed, slipping the weapon under her pillow. He accidentally wakes her up as he retrieves the gun, and she tells him that she has been dreaming that something is chasing after her.

THE CREEPER, 1948

542 Hello Dolly!

Mad scientist Marcel shows Lavond a tiny dog in his laboratory. Lavond assumes it is a toy and is shocked to learn that it is a real dog shrunk to one-sixth of its normal size, "Eight hours ago it was a full-grown Saint Bernard!" Lavond soon realizes that he can use Marcel's miniaturizing techniques to his own advantage.

THE DEVIL DOLL, 1936

543 Be furious and do it fast...

A white Jaguar speeds along a winding road, pulls in at a diner, and an attractive blonde gets out. In the diner, a truck driver tells her about an escaped murderer called Webster that everyone is looking for. The camera moves to a silent dark-haired man sitting alone at the end of the counter. He looks out the window at the Jaguar, listening to every word they say...

THE FAST AND THE FURIOUS, 1954

544 Grim reaper

Evelyn finds her daughter's gerbil while working in her garden and stabs the little animal with her sickle. She then goes into the house, where her daughter Lori is holding a séance. She is trying to contact her dead father: "It's Mama. She's getting sick again." Evelyn is poised behind the girl with her sickle in her hands as Lori speaks to the spirits: "Show me a sign."

MOUNTAINTOP MOTEL MASSACRE, 1986

545 Melvin was a 90lb weakling until nuclear waste transformed him into...The Toxic Avenger!

A cruel prank leads to janitor Melvin kissing a sheep while dressed in a pink tutu! Running away from his laughing tormentors, he falls into a drum of toxic waste. He climbs out and runs off in a blaze of fire to plan his revenge...

THE TOXIC AVENGER, 1985

546 The desert is a very big place

Leather-clad gunslinger El Topo is riding through the desert with his seven-year-old son when they come upon the scene of a massacre. A dying man tells them who is responsible for the carnage, fueling El Topo's rage. Soon, all he can think about is revenge.

EL TOPO, 1970

547 The land where monsters live!

Professor Challenger stands in front of explorers, hunters, and journalists at the Zoological Institute and claims to have made an astonishing discovery: on an isolated plateau in the Amazon, he saw live dinosaurs! When he is called a liar, the professor proposes taking a new expedition to the Amazon...

THE LOST WORLD, 1960

548 People are croaking all over the place

Pickett, Karen, and the children escape from the massing frogs by canoe. They are attacked by snakes and alligators, but they manage to reach the other bank and hitch a ride in a passing car. The boy in the car wants to show them something he picked up at camp; suddenly they hear the familiar "ribbit, ribbit."

FROGS, 1972

549 "They're smarter than all of us put together."

When a flying saucer lands near a small town, the U.S. military moves in quickly to hush it up, because "civilization itself" depends on absolute security. They aren't quick enough, though, and a young couple runs over a strange alien creature with their car.

THE EYE CREATURES, 1965

550 "I'm Kabukiman!"

At a Kabuki performance, one of the performers suddenly starts killing the rest of the cast. New York cop Harry Griswold grabs his gun and tries to intervene, but once on stage he is surprised when a dying old man kisses him…Griswold is now possessed by the spirit of a great Kabuki master and must do battle with "the evil one."

SGT. KABUKIMAN N.Y.P.D. 1991

A Good
Night In

Thanks to DVDs, videos, and pay-per-view television, these days we can watch almost any movie, from any era or genre, at any time, from the comfort of our own homes. Whether you want to snuggle up on the couch with your sweetheart, enjoy a girls' night in front of the latest romantic comedy, or catch the latest action flick with the guys, there are plenty of wonderful movies to choose from. You may not get the thrill of the big screen experience, but you can still enjoy a great movie and "a good night in."

Previous page: Vivien Leigh and Hattie McDaniel in
Gone with the Wind (1939).

551 "Sometimes there's so much beauty in the world, I feel like I can't take it, like my heart's going to cave in."

This movie is full of beautifully cinematic and memorable moments, including the scene in which Lester (Kevin Spacey) first meets Angela (Mena Suvari) at the basketball game. He begins to fantasize about the beautiful young cheerleader, and he imagines her slowly and seductively unzipping her top, releasing a cascade of rose petals.

AMERICAN BEAUTY, 1999

552 Patriotic friends

A group of friends gathers around a dining table to mourn their dead comrade. George Dzunda fights back his tears as he scrambles eggs in the kitchen, and he starts to hum "God Bless America." Meryl Streep joins in, and then the others follow suit in an eerie but poignant chorus.

THE DEER HUNTER, 1978

553 1500 miles is a long way home

In this marvelous true story, three Australian aborigine girls escape from a government camp and set out on a grueling 1500-mile journey across the outback to their home. In one great scene, the girls put their skills at finding water to the test.

RABBIT-PROOF FENCE, 2002

554 Flying without wings

Jack helps Rose to climb onto the rail at the prow of the huge ship, and he stretches her arms out to the side. As she opens her eyes, Rose gasps, "I'm flying!"

TITANIC, 1997

555 Simply charming

In the beautiful final scene of this movie, the three Waterbury children are reunited with their father at the railway station. Bobbie recognizes him through the engine steam and runs along the platform, calling, "My Daddy...my Daddy!"

THE RAILWAY CHILDREN, 1970

556 "Hello, and welcome to another day of higher education!"

Jena Hoeman whispers something to one of the popular, but bitchy girls in her gym class. The gym teacher hears her whispering and asks her to repeat what she'd said:

Jena: "I hope they shrivel up and fall off."
Teacher: "You hope what shrivels up and falls off?"
Jena: "Her breasts, Miss Deeds."

PRETTY IN PINK, 1986

557 The cold war just got hotter

As he stalks a Russian submarine, warship captain Eric Finlander loudly tells a reporter that he knows his duty, and that "if he fires one, I'll fire one." The crew is extremely tense, and they only hear Finlander say "fire one." The missile controller, his finger on the crucial red button, reacts immediately...

THE BEDFORD INCIDENT, 1965

558 Schmidt happens

Retired widower Warren Schmidt tries to talk his daughter out of her impending marriage to Randall Hertzel by describing a dream to her: "There was a…well, it wasn't really a spaceship, it was more like a blimp, or an orb of some kind. And then a bunch of weird creatures came out and started trying to take you away, and you wanna know what? They all looked like Randall. Do you understand? And I was jumping up and down to save you."

ABOUT SCHMIDT, 2002

559 Hold your breath

This movie literally had its viewers holding their breath as they watched divers competing to submerge themselves ever deeper in seawater on only lungfuls of air. With each dive scene, the relief felt as the characters break the surface once more and suck in huge gulps of fresh air becomes increasingly palpable.

THE BIG BLUE, 1988

560 A beautiful demise

In the final scene, Dirk Bogarde sits in a deck chair on an Italian beach that is dotted with striped bathing tents. The dark dye from his hair runs down his face with the beads of sweat his cholera fever produces. He sees a youthful male figure striking a classical pose at the water's edge—a true celebration of death.

DEATH IN VENICE, 1971

561 What he really wanted was to spend Thanksgiving with his family. What he got was three days with the turkey.

In one funny scene, Neal Page (Steve Martin) and Del Griffith (John Candy) have to share a bed, and they accidentally start cuddling during the night. Neal wakes, confused, and asks Del where his hand is. Del sleepily answers, "Between two pillows." Neal quickly jumps out of bed, shouting, "Those aren't pillows!"

PLANES, TRAINS AND AUTOMOBILES, 1987

562 The damage is done

Richard Bone finally manages to seduce Mo Cutter, his best friend's wife. Thinking that Mo is asleep, he leaves her during the night, but Mo is not asleep, and the look on her face says it all: betrayal.

CUTTER'S WAY, 1981

563 Anything but...

In one unforgettable scene, Marilyn Monroe uses a collection of toys, torches, and balloons to demonstrate the theory of relativity to Albert Einstein!

INSIGNIFICANCE, 1985

564 "Thank you for coming back to me."

At the end of this bittersweet tearjerker, Laura returns from her romantic dreams to her life with her husband, to the sound of Rachmaninov's *Piano Concerto No. 2*.

BRIEF ENCOUNTER, 1945

565 They took a bite out of crime

Ray Winkler (Woody Allen) is a terrible crook with big dreams. As he struggles to find his way through a basement tunnel he'd dug to rob the bank next door, his wife is upstairs, selling cookies in the store they'd opened as a cover for their planned crime—and she's making millions!

SMALL TIME CROOKS, 2000

566 The last post

It is the year 2013, and a monumental war has devastated the earth and drastically reduced the population of the United States, which has been left ungoverned. A drifter by the name of Gordon Krantz stumbles upon a jeep. Inside it is a postman—dead. He buries the body and takes the man's uniform and mailbag.

THE POSTMAN, 1997

567 "Here's looking at you, kid."

Humphrey Bogart and Ingrid Bergman's farewell at the airport will always be an utterly unforgettable movie moment: "It doesn't take much to see that the problems of three little people don't amount to a hill of beans in this crazy world. Someday you'll understand that. Here's looking at you, kid."

CASABLANCA, 1942

568 There are some places in the universe you don't go alone

The surviving marines argue over who will risk their lives by going outside to contact the ship. The android Bishop quietly and reluctantly says, "I'll go." Ripley is impressed by his self-sacrifice, and he candidly remarks, "Believe me, I'd prefer not to. I may be synthetic but I'm not stupid."

ALIENS, 1986

569 He knows no fear
He knows no danger
He knows nothing

Inept secret agent Johnny English is in charge of security at the funeral of Agent One. The head of British Intelligence stops at the entrance to the cemetery and asks, "Everything in order, English?" Just as English tells him, "You are now entering the most secure place in the whole of England," there is a huge explosion behind him...

JOHNNY ENGLISH, 2003

570 This time he's fighting for his life

Vietnam veteran Sylvester Stallone wanders into a small Oregon town to get some food, but the town's sheriff takes one look at him and decides he wants him out. The sheriff drives Stallone out of town across the bridge, throws him an ironic salute, and drives away. Stallone looks from the mountains to the bridge, pulls his collar up, turns around, and walks decisively back into town...

FIRST BLOOD, 1982

571 To enter the mind of a killer, she must challenge the mind of a madman.

At the end of the movie, Hannibal Lecter speaks to Clarice Starling on the phone. He watches his former prison warden getting off of a plane, smiles, and cheerfully tells Clarice, "You'll have to excuse me. I'm having an old friend for dinner."

THE SILENCE OF THE LAMBS, 1991

572 "I never knew it could be like this! Nobody ever kissed me the way you do."

The iconic moment in this movie is the clinch between Burt Lancaster and Deborah Kerr, as the waves crash over them on a beach at sunset.

FROM HERE TO ETERNITY, 1953

573 "I'm back, baby!"

Secret agent Austin Powers backflips through colorful sets into a crowd of extras, opens his arms to the audience, and welcomes us back with his huge, yellow-toothed grin.

AUSTIN POWERS IN GOLDMEMBER, 2002

574 He's quite engaging
She's otherwise engaged

After helping Andie MacDowell to choose her wedding dress, Hugh Grant tries to find the words to express his feelings for her: "I…I just wondered…er…I really feel, er, in short, to recap it slightly in a clearer version…um, the words of David Cassidy, in fact, er, while he was still with the Partridge family, er, I think I love you."

FOUR WEDDINGS AND A FUNERAL, 1993

575 Being wild
is in their blood

Sam is on the phone to his mom when he sees his brother floating outside his bedroom window:
Sam: "You're a vampire!"
Michael: "No, I'm not!"
Sam: "Then who are you? The Flying Nun?!"
THE LOST BOYS, 1987

576 Surrender pronto, or we'll level Toronto!

Sheriff Boomer, Kabral, and Roy Boy steal a truck and paint anti-Canadian graffiti all over it. Later, they are pulled over by a motorcycle cop, who tells them that the graffiti on their truck must be written in both English *and* French.

CANADIAN BACON, 1995

577 No more mister nice guy

In a rare performance as a villain, Henry Fonda makes a dramatic entrance—as the sweeping musical score gets our adrenaline pumping, he appears out of the dust with his gang, having just murdered rancher Brett McBain and his children.

ONCE UPON A TIME IN THE WEST, 1969

578 It's about flights of fantasy. And the nightmare of reality.

Amid the futuristic mayhem, technological chaos, and meddling bureaucracy, one middle-management worker fantasizes about soaring on mechanical wings toward a woman in the clouds.

BRAZIL, 1985

579 You will believe

Reluctant psychic Oda Mae is ghost Sam's only hope of contacting his girlfriend, Molly. But Oda Mae doesn't want to be able to hear the dead, and Sam becomes frustrated when she tries to ignore him:

Sam: "God dammit—"

Oda Mae: "Don't you 'God dammit' me. Don't you take the Lord's name in vain with me. I don't take that!"

Sam: "Would you relax?"

Oda Mae: "No, you relax! You're the dead guy!"

GHOST, 1990

580 A nervous romance

Woody Allen gets fed up listening to two obnoxious people behind him argue about the meaning of Marshall McLuhan's work. He resolves the argument by stepping out of the cinema line, and then out of frame. He returns with McLuhan himself, who speaks directly to the camera and sets everyone straight.

ANNIE HALL, 1977

581 Getting to know you

Elliott has a close encounter with a creature in his backyard—even playing ball games with it. He knows that something is out there and he runs into the house, hyped up, to tell his family what happened.

Michael: "Maybe it was an iguana."

Elliott: "It was *no* iguana."

Michael: "You know how they say there are alligators in the sewers?"

Gertie: "Alligators in the sewers."

Mary: "All we're trying to say is, maybe you just probably imagined it."

Elliott: "I couldn't have imagined it!"

E.T. THE EXTRA-TERRESTRIAL, 1982

582 "Everyone knows diaries are just full of crap."

Wearing only a sweater and her underwear, Bridget Jones chases after Mark Darcy to explain that she didn't mean the things she had written about him in her diary. As the reunited couple embrace and kiss in the snow, Bridget remarks, "Wait a minute, nice boys don't kiss like that." Darcy replies, "Oh yes, they f***ing do," and he pulls her closer for another kiss.

BRIDGET JONES'S DIARY, 2001

583 "Slippery little suckers"

At an important dinner meeting, call girl Julia Roberts has difficulties eating her escargots (snails). One she is wrestling with flies off of her tongs into the air and is deftly caught by a waiter.

PRETTY WOMAN, 1990

584 Damp spirits

In the opening scenes of this movie, the grief, isolation, and loneliness felt by widower George Clooney are made almost palpable by the terrific, drifting soundtrack that accompanies him as he walks through the rain-soaked streets.

SOLARIS, 2002

585 One for the nest

Matthew Modine and Nicholas Cage both return scarred from the Vietnam War. Cage's wounds are physical, but Modine's are mental—he yearns to be a bird. In the surprising but stunning final scene, he manages to fulfill his fantasy...

BIRDY, 1984

586 Fountain of youth

There is one scene that perfectly reiterates the title of the film. While the paparazzi snap photos, the glorious goddess Sylvia (Anita Ekberg) bathes playfully in the cascading waters of the famous Trevi Fountain, as journalist Marcello Rubini (Marcello Mastroianni) gazes at her with adoring puppy-dog eyes.

LA DOLCE VITA, 1960

587 The battle for Middle-earth begins!

Aragorn and Gimli the Dwarf go through the secret door at the foot of Helm's Deep to surprise the enemy that is attacking the main gate. They look at the bridge they have to reach:

Gimli: "Toss me!"

Aragorn: "What!"

Gimli: "I cannot jump the distance. You'll have to toss me. Don't tell the Elf!"

THE LORD OF THE RINGS: THE TWO TOWERS, 2002

588 The turning of the tides

In a rain-swept Greek town, the forces of right-wing religion, represented by hundreds of handheld torches, clash with the forces of liberated culture, represented by pitch-black umbrellas. As the right attacks, the tide goes out for the sea of umbrellas.

ULYSSES' GAZE, 1995

589 "It's just the way I see things."

This movie ends where it began, with Noodles lying on a mattress in an opium den, smoking a pipe, a mysterious and enigmatic smile on his face.

ONCE UPON A TIME IN AMERICA, 1984

590 The most magnificent picture ever!

The passionate kiss between Rhett Butler and Scarlett O'Hara, with Atlanta burning behind them is simply breathtaking.

GONE WITH THE WIND, 1939

591 He's a cop with the odds against him...it's time to even the score.

In the chilling final scene, obsessive detective Lloyd Hopkins corners a serial killer in a school gym. The killer knows he is caught, and he says, "You're a cop, and you gotta take me in." But Lloyd has a different idea of justice in mind: "I got some good news and some bad news..." The screen goes black. We hear two gunshots, then the sound of spent cartridges hitting the floor...

COP, 1988

592 Frothy coffee

Young Amélie (Audrey Tautou) is determined to help other people find love. In the café where she works, she has lit the fuse between a regular customer and the woman who works at the cigarette counter and now they have slipped into the lavatory together! Amélie tries desperately to cover up their noisy bumps and squeals of pleasure by setting the coffee machine at full speed.

AMÉLIE, 2001

593 "We commit your final mortal remains to the bosom of the Pacific Ocean…"

Jeffrey "the Dude" Lebowski and Walter stand on the edge of a cliff, paying their last respects to Donny. As Walter throws Donny's ashes into the sea, a sudden gust of wind blows them right back into the Dude's face.

THE BIG LEBOWSKI, 1998

594 Don't lose your head

The mysterious killer wields an enormous surgical bonecutter as he approaches a night nurse in the quiet hospital corridor. We are not actually shown what happens to her, but the brief shot of a headless statue gives us a good clue!

THE EXORCIST III, 1990

595 What one loves about life are the things that fade

In one beautifully romantic scene, the band begins to play after all the other dancers have left, and Kris Kristofferson and Isabelle Huppert waltz around the empty ballroom.

HEAVEN'S GATE, 1980

596 It could happen to you

Gil Buckman is with his ill daughter in the bedroom. He asks her if she wants to throw up. "OK," she says, and does—all over him. When his wife comes in, he is still standing there, dumbfounded. He remarks, "I'm just waitin' for her head to spin around!"

PARENTHOOD, 1989

597 Love means never having to say you're sorry

The poignant scene when young Jenny (Ali McGraw) dies in husband Oliver's (Ryan O'Neal) arms will continue to have audiences in floods of tears for years to come.

LOVE STORY, 1970

598 Any requests?

After his death, Jack's three oldest friends and his foster son take his ashes on a memorable journey to fulfill his "last orders" by scattering them into the sea. When they finally reach their destination, the camera draws silently back from the moving scene.

LAST ORDERS, 2001

599
She makes dinner. She does windows. She reads bedtime stories. She's a blessing...in disguise.

Daniel Hillard (Robin Williams), disguised as housekeeper Mrs. Doubtfire, reaches over the stove to get the salt and pepper shakers, and his fake breasts catch on fire. He puts out the fire with two pot lids and says, "I've only been a woman for a day and already I'm getting hot flushes!"

MRS. DOUBTFIRE, 1993

600
Yule crack up!

The Griswolds' plans for a traditional family Christmas become a disaster when all the family arrives. In one amusing scene, Aunt Bethany sits by the Christmas tree and asks what that squeaky noise is. Uncle Lewis replies, "You couldn't hear a dump truck drive through a nitroglycerin plant."

NATIONAL LAMPOON'S CHRISTMAS VACATION, 1989

Fantasy

Fantasy films are our tickets to unreality, to the land of make-believe, where the impossible becomes possible and the strange visions of our dreams come to life. Often based on traditional myths, legends, and fairy tales, these movies can feature any magical place, character, or story that the writers conjure up. These wondrous movies appeal to adults and children alike, which makes them excellent family films for rainy days. No matter how old we are, we can still enjoy the excitement of a ride on a flying carpet, a visit from a ghost, or a journey to the center of the earth.

Previous page: Malcolm McDowell in *A Clockwork Orange* (1971).

601 "We swears to serve the master of the Precious."

Having tracked the Hobbits for days, Gollum becomes their guide to Mount Doom. The creature becomes increasingly disturbed—part of him wants to help his master, Frodo, and part of him yearns for the ring, his "Precious." His internal conflict becomes an intense battle between his former self, Smeagol, and his new, evil self, Gollum:

Gollum: "You must kill Master."
Smeagol: "But Master is our friend."
Gollum: "You don't have any friends!"

THE LORD OF THE RINGS: THE TWO TOWERS, 2002

602 Now! The story that has brought joy to millions! A new screen triumph!

Bitter old miser Ebenezer Scrooge is en route to learning the error of his ways through some ghostly intervention. He has already endured the lessons of the Ghost of Christmas Past when the huge and boisterous Ghost of Christmas Present pays him an unwelcome visit:

Ghost: "You've never seen the likes of me before, have you?"
Scrooge: "Never, and I wish the pleasure had been indefinitely postponed."

SCROOGE, 1951

603 Learning can be magic

To avoid the bombardment of letters that have been arriving by courier owls from Hogwarts School, Harry spends his birthday—thanks to his wicked guardians—in a remote lighthouse. In the middle of the night, a friendly, hairy giant emerges from the storm, armed with a birthday cake and a letter, to rescue Harry and show him his destiny: "You're a wizard, Harry!"

HARRY POTTER AND THE SORCERER'S STONE, 2001

604 Wonderful musical adventure

When Jonathan the woodcutter spares a special tree, the magical Forest Queen grants his and his wife's greatest wish. They become the proud parents of a son. A very, very small son. A son the size of your thumb.

TOM THUMB, 1958

605 Hold onto your breath!

Seaman Ned Land (Kirk Douglas) is captured by Captain Nemo and taken aboard his *Nautilus* submarine in this Jules Verne epic, which has an exciting scene of a battle being waged against a giant squid.

20,000 LEAGUES UNDER THE SEA, 1954

606 Makes *Ben-Hur* look like an epic!

King Arthur and his knights make an unforgettable entrance, not on horseback, but by prancing around as if on imaginary horses, with their servants providing horse-hoof sound effects by banging coconut shells together.

MONTY PYTHON AND THE HOLY GRAIL, 1975

607 A colossus of adventure!

Jason manages to discover the Golden Fleece, but before he can obtain his prize, he must defeat a seven-headed hydra and an army of resurrected, skeleton soldiers that have been summoned by Aetes!

JASON AND THE ARGONAUTS, 1963

608 "He who draws the sword from the stone, he shall be king."

In this lavish production about King Arthur, the knights of the Round Table, Merlin's wizardry, and the quest for the Holy Grail, it comes down to basics in the great moment when young Arthur magically pulls the sword Excalibur from the stone, when everyone before him has failed.

EXCALIBUR, 1981

609 Where everything seems possible and nothing is what it seems

Angry that she has to look after her brother Toby, Sarah wishes that the goblins would come and take him away—and they do! The Goblin King, Jareth, explains to Sarah that Toby will be transformed into a goblin unless she can find her way to his castle: "You have 13 hours in which to solve the labyrinth, before your baby brother becomes one of us—forever."

LABYRINTH, 1986

610 Trust means everything

When a jolly, elderly man named Kris Kringle stands in for a drunken department-store Santa, he provokes media mayhem by insisting that he is the real Santa Claus. Some want him locked away as a lunatic, and only an extremely clever lawyer can get him off. In the courtroom, the tension is thick as a little girl presents the judge with a one-dollar bill and the lawyer asks the court to consider four little words printed on the back of it: In God We Trust.

MIRACLE ON 34TH STREET, 1994

611 Fancy footwork

In a magical world of dancing princesses, elves, and dragons, there is a marvelous gypsy dance, which features stimulating moves from Russ Tamblyn as the woodsman.

THE WONDERFUL WORLD OF THE BROTHERS GRIMM, 1962

612 It's a long way down...

Newly knighted Professor Oliver Lindenbrook is given a piece of lava by his class. Examining the stone, they discover, concealed deep inside it, a geologist's plumb bob with Icelandic inscriptions written upon it. The message describes the route explorer Arne Saknussemm traveled to the interior of the earth.

JOURNEY TO THE CENTER OF THE EARTH, 1959

613 Cowboys battle monsters in the lost world

A cowboy travels to a hidden valley in Mexico to capture a living dinosaur. He meets with fantastic prehistoric creatures—courtesy of stop-motion animator Ray Harryhausen—and, in one groundbreaking cinema moment, we watch him feed one with a sugar cube.

THE VALLEY OF GWANGI, 1969

614 The story of an uncommonly gentle man

In Tim Burton's poignant tale, Edward, a likeable and innocent young man with a Gothic appearance and scissors where his fingers should be, is adopted into a small community, where his talents for topiary and haircutting quickly become evident.

EDWARD SCISSORHANDS, 1990

615 One wife too many

A happily married author invites an eccentric medium to dinner as research for one of his novels. They hold a séance, and the ghost of his first wife, Elvira, appears, and then refuses to go away.

BLITHE SPIRIT, 1945

616 Orbit into the fantastic future!

It's 1899. George steps into his new machine and is thrust forward in time. He is distressed to see two world wars, then a huge nuclear explosion. He is entombed in his time machine as it continues further forward in time, until he arrives at the year 802,701 and what appears to be an idyllic world populated by gentle people…

THE TIME MACHINE, 1960

617 Ever wanted to be someone else? Now you can.

Puppeteer Craig Schwartz discovers a mysterious portal that leads directly into the head of actor John Malkovich. When Craig turns the portal into a business venture, Malkovich finds out what is going on and is none too pleased:

Craig Schwartz: "Mr. Malkovich, Sir, with all due respect, I discovered that portal. It's my livelihood"

John Malkovich: "It's my head, Schwartz. It's my head!"

BEING JOHN MALKOVICH, 1999

618 They saw him coming

In a world where even everyday mundane tasks require paperwork in triplicate, Sam Lowry is astounded by his welcome at the Information Retrieval department.

Porter: "Thirtieth floor, sir. You're expected."

Sam Lowry: "Um…don't you want to search me?"

Porter: "No, sir."

Sam Lowry: "Do you want to see my ID?"

Porter: "No need, sir."

Sam Lowry: "But I could be anybody."

Porter: "No you couldn't, sir. This is Information Retrieval."

BRAZIL, 1985

619 "If you build it, he will come."

Controversial 1960s writer Terence Mann is amazed to see the ghosts of great baseball players of the past playing in Ray Kinsella's cornfield, but he understands the magic and importance of what he sees: "The one constant through all the years, Ray, has been baseball. America has rolled by like an army of steamrollers. It's been erased like a blackboard, rebuilt, and erased again. But baseball has marked the time. This field, this game, is a part of our past, Ray. It reminds us of all that once was good, and that could be again. Oh people will come, Ray. People will most definitely come."

FIELD OF DREAMS, 1989

620 Heart of darkness...

In this bleak fantasy, Captain Willard (Martin Sheen) is on a mission to take out the mad renegade Colonel Kurtz (Marlon Brando). He arrives at Kurtz's compound to find that all order has disappeared, and that the soldiers and natives live tribally under their godlike chief.

Kurtz: "Are you an assassin?"

Willard: "I'm a soldier."

Kurtz: "You're neither. You're an errand boy, sent by grocery clerks to collect a bill."

APOCALYPSE NOW, 1979

294

621 Pale by comparison, but enough to make any man blush

Private detective Eddie Valiant is surprised to see black-and-white cartoon star Betty Boop selling cigarettes at the Ink and Paint Club:

Eddie Valiant: "What are you doin' here?"

Betty Boop: "Well, it's been kinda slow since cartoons went to color. But I still got it, Eddie. Boop boop be-doop!"

Eddie Valiant: "Yeah, you still got it."

WHO FRAMED ROGER RABBIT, 1988

622 Being the adventures of a young man whose principal interests are rape, ultraviolence, and Beethoven.

An overture plays, and the camera pans down from a gilded proscenium above the stage of a derelict theater, a symbol of collapsed civilization. Over the music, we hear the screams of a young woman struggling in the clutches of five delinquents, who wear the remnants of old Nazi uniforms. In a voice-over, Alex explains: "It was around by the derelict casino that we came across Billyboy and his four droogs. They were getting ready to perform a little of the old in–out, in–out on a weepy young devotchka they had there."

A CLOCKWORK ORANGE, 1971

623 Only a rose...

A poor merchant, lost in the forest, enters a strange castle. He sees a beautiful rose and picks it up as a gift for his daughter. Then the castle's owner appears. He is half-human, half-beast, with magical powers, and he sentences the merchant to death, unless one of his daughters replaces him...

BEAUTY AND THE BEAST, 1946

624 Bolt the doors! Lock the windows! Dr. Lao's coming to town!

In this strange comedy-western, a mysterious, old traveling showman who leads a life guided by ancient philosophies transforms himself into a variety of beings, including a giant, talking serpent.

SEVEN FACES OF DR. LAO, 1964

625 Shell-shocked

Doctor Gulliver discovers that the king of the Lilliputians wishes to use him as a weapon in their war against their enemies, who break their eggs from the wrong end—it's the battle of the Big Enders versus the Little Enders!

THE 3 WORLDS OF GULLIVER, 1960

626 Remarkable. Unbelievable. Impossible. And true.

This movie is crammed with wonderful scenes about the notorious teller of tall tales. In one, we are treated to his adventures with the headless King of the Moon, played by the excellent Robin Williams.

THE ADVENTURES OF BARON MUNCHAUSEN, 1988

627 They're making memories tonight!

An angel named Clarence falls to earth to show a broken and suicidal businessman what life in his hometown would have been like if he had never existed: "One man's life touches so many others, when he's not there it leaves an awfully big hole."

IT'S A WONDERFUL LIFE, 1946

628 Deep below the blue surface, there lies a place no one has ever dreamed of...

Lindsey and Bud are trapped in a mini-submersible that is rapidly filling with water on the sea floor. With only one air tank between them, they must make a very difficult decision in order to survive. Lindsey will have to drown, and Bud will have to pull her back to the main vessel and try to resuscitate her there...

THE ABYSS, 1989

629 A world beyond imagination!

At the height of the American Civil War, Union captain Cyrus Harding, a young war reporter, and a former slave are being held captive in a Confederate prison. They make their escape during a battle by stealing the giant weather balloon stationed in the camp, but they sail straight into the clutches of "the greatest hurricane ever seen by man," which blows them toward a mysterious island…

MYSTERIOUS ISLAND, 1961

630 He's having the worst day of his life…over and over…

Weatherman Phil Connors is sent on a job he hates—to cover a story about a groundhog that can predict the weather. He wakes up on Groundhog Day to the sound of Sonny and Cher playing on the radio alarm clock, and he reluctantly heads into town and does his report. The next morning, Phil awakens with a strong sense of déjà vu. He hears a familiar song on the radio—and is horrified to learn that it is Groundhog Day all over again!

GROUNDHOG DAY, 1993

631 Past meets present

When modern-day astronauts arrive on the moon, they find evidence that someone was there before them—an eccentric Victorian inventor had developed an antigravity material and traveled to the moon, claiming it in the name of Queen Victoria!

FIRST MEN IN THE MOON, 1964

632 Golden slumber

When one of Sinbad's sailors shoots a bat-winged creature flying over their ship, it drops a strange gold medallion, which Sinbad ties around his neck. He then starts having strange dreams of an evil man in black and a dancing girl with an eye tattooed on her palm!

THE GOLDEN VOYAGE OF SINBAD, 1973

633 The greatest adventure a man ever lived!

A British pilot, who cheats death by falling in love with an American girl over the radio before jumping out of his burning plane, goes to court in Heaven to argue for his life. Meanwhile, he undergoes emergency brain surgery on Earth, while his newfound love watches.

A MATTER OF LIFE AND DEATH, 1946

634 The end is just the beginning

Although loving mother Annie Nielson has been severely affected by the deaths of her two children and her husband in separate car accidents, her character and spirit still shine through: "A whole family lost to car crashes. It's enough to make a person buy a bike."

WHAT DREAMS MAY COME, 1998

635 On waves of song, laughter, and romance!

See this wonderful movie if only to catch Gene Kelly's magical live-action dance scene with Jerry, the animated mouse from the *Tom and Jerry* cartoons!

ANCHORS AWEIGH, 1945

636 The space-age adventuress whose sexploits are among the most bizarre ever seen

Jane Fonda, in the title role, drifts through the galaxy, getting in and out of trouble as often as she gets in and out of bed! In one scene, the villain straps her into a machine that is supposed to ravage her, but she takes great delight in the experience and wears out the machine, commenting, "This is really much too poetic a way to die."

BARBARELLA, 1968

637 They didn't make history, they stole it!

Kevin hears a noise in the dark and sees a flickering light under his closet door. Something suddenly comes crashing through the door and into his bedroom—it is a clumsy band of renegade dwarves who have stolen a map of the universe's wormholes and are traveling through time looting whatever treasure they can find—but they are being pursued by the Supreme Being, who wants his map back!

TIME BANDITS, 1981

638 Fantasia will amazia!

Disney animators worked to classical music, performed by the Philadelphia Orchestra, to create this enchanting masterpiece. A personal favorite is "The Sorcerer's Apprentice," which stars Mickey Mouse as an aspiring magician who oversteps his capabilities.

FANTASIA, 1940

639 "Whistle while you work"

Armed with pickaxes, shovels, and lanterns, seven men form a procession to march to work. Doc, Grumpy, Happy, Sleepy, Sneezy, Bashful, and Dopey—seven dwarfs—trundle through the woods, singing, "Hi ho, hi ho, it's off to work we go…"

SNOW WHITE AND THE SEVEN DWARFS, 1937

640 Spring of youth

Three elderly pals regularly sneak onto private property to swim, but it has been rented by a man named Walter, who brings large pods back from the sea and leaves them submerged in the pool. When the guys see the strange pods, they wonder if it is safe to go into the pool, but decide to risk it. They dive into the water and come out feeling rejuvenated and full of youthful vigor.

COCOON, 1985

641 A little pig goes a long way

In a rousing finale, the sheepherding pig named Babe wins the prestigious National Sheepdog Championships. His owner, Farmer Hoggett, gives him a friendly look and simply says, "That'll do, pig, that'll do."

BABE, 1995

642 Beyond the horizon lies the secret to a new beginning

The mutant Mariner tries to make it clear to his unwanted passenger, Helen, that the strange markings on a young girl's back do not mark the way to dry land: "Dry land is a myth!" He soon realizes that the only way to prove it to her is to show her, so he grabs some flares and takes Helen deeper and deeper under the water…

WATERWORLD, 1995

643 **Haven't you ever dreamed of a place where there was peace and security, where living was not a struggle, but a lasting delight?**

A plane runs out of fuel and crashes into deep snow in the Himalayan Mountains. The survivors fear that all is lost, until they are rescued by a strange, soft-spoken Chinese man, who leads them, tethered together, across miles of difficult terrain to a small pass, where they find themselves in the closest place to Heaven on Earth.

LOST HORIZON, 1937

644 **Cut**

Blink and you'll miss the decomposing donkey being dragged along on top of a grand piano, in Luis Buñuel and Salvador Dali's surrealist film.

UN CHIEN ANDALOU, 1929

645 **Things that go bump in the night**

When Lucy Muir meets the ghost of Captain Gregg in her new home, he only allows her to stay because she puts his portrait up in the bedroom. Modesty drives her to cover it with a small quilt while she undresses for bed. She positions her hot-water bottle, fluffs the pillow, and blows out the lamp. She then hears the captain's voice say, "My dear! Never let anyone tell you to be ashamed of your figure."

THE GHOST AND MRS. MUIR, 1947

646 You will believe...

A dragon-slayer called Bowen realizes that his livelihood is in jeopardy when the last surviving dragon, Draco, asks him, "When there are no more dragons to slay, how will you make a living, knight?" The two decide to travel together, and devise a clever trick—the dragon will scare the populace and Bowen will pretend to slay him, and collect large rewards from the grateful towns.

DRAGONHEART, 1996

647 The future looks bleak

A small German town hosts a traveling fair, at which Dr. Caligari exhibits Cesare, a somnambulist who can predict the future. The crowd visiting the tent is shown Cesare in his state of eternal sleep. Caligari commands him to wake. His darkened eyelids flutter open and he emerges from his trance, rising from his coffin and taking a few steps. From the crowd, a man named Alan asks, "How long have I to live?" Cesare's immediate response is, "Until dawn."

THE CABINET OF DR. CALIGARI, 1919

648 You'll believe a man can fly!

Christopher Reeve is fantastic as the Man of Steel. The most memorable moments are the flying scenes, which really do make it appear as though the famous, caped hero can fly better than a bird, as he soars above the streets of Metropolis with his love, Lois Lane.

SUPERMAN: THE MOVIE, 1978

649 News to melt your heart

This movie is one for the whole family. Papa and Santa Claus finally break the news to Papa's adopted son, Buddy, who is over 6 feet tall and is lousy at toy-making, that he is not really an elf. He has a real, human father living in New York—and Papa and Santa Claus think that Buddy should seek him out.

ELF, 2003

650 Some people follow their dreams. Others steal them.

Demented scientist Krank is unable to dream, so he tries to steal children's dreams. However, he doesn't consider that all children fear him, and he soon discovers that he is only able to get their nightmares.

THE CITY OF LOST CHILDREN, 1995

Musicals

Of course there was no such thing as a musical before sound was introduced to film in the late 1920s, but since then there's been no turning back! These quirky projects had their golden age in the '30s and '40s, but have recently proved their staying power with the tremendous success of *Moulin Rouge!* and *Chicago*. Musicals combine music, dance, song, and choreography with a variety of story lines, but they often offer fantastic, escapist, and upbeat stories involving a search for love or success. As the stakes hot up in the area of action thrillers and FX movies, it's good to know that there is always another musical in the pipeline.

Previous page: Bert Lahr, Jack Haley, Judy Garland, and Ray Bolger in *The Wizard of Oz* (1939).

651 The happiest sound in all the world!

No one who has ever seen this film could possibly forget the wonderful opening crane shot of Julie Andrews running across the mountaintop singing "The Hills Are Alive."

THE SOUND OF MUSIC, 1965

652 "High flying, adored"

A large crowd calls from below: "Evita…Evita!" Eva Peron comes to the balcony, and silence descends. She addresses her people via the enormously sentimental number "Don't Cry for Me Argentina."

EVITA, 1996

653 Ambushed

Fashion-magazine editor Maggie Prescott (Kay Thompson) and photographer Dick Avery (Fred Astaire) descend on a gloomy bookstore in Greenwich Village to try to add an air of intelligence to their latest photo shoot. Store clerk Jo Stockton (Audrey Hepburn) is appalled when they ambush her little shop with an army of pink-clad assistants and she asks them to leave. But she is abruptly dismissed and thrown out, and she can only watch in horror as they run riot among her precious books.

FUNNY FACE, 1957

654 Brush up on your Shakespeare

Divorced actors Fred and Lilly are brought back together by Cole Porter to star in his musical version of Shakespeare's *The Taming of the Shrew*. The couple have a lot in common with their Shakespearian characters Petruchio and Katherine, and when a fight breaks out on opening night, it threatens the whole production.

KISS ME KATE, 1953

655 "Dear little village, little town of mine."

In a small Jewish village in Russia, news arrives via the constable that all the villagers must sell their homes and leave within three days. As the people think about their futures, they come together to sing a poignant song about their home, "Anatevka."

FIDDLER ON THE ROOF, 1971

656 "More?!"

Starving young orphan Oliver Twist slowly makes his way through the orphanage dining hall, holds his little bowl out in front of him, and bravely says, "Please, sir, I want some more."

OLIVER! 1968

657 What a joy!

Jerry Mulligan appears to be the only guest at Milo's party. He admires the elegant heiress's one-shouldered white gown in one of the film's most famous lines, "That's, uh, quite a dress you almost have on. What holds it up?" To which she cleverly replies, "Modesty!"

AN AMERICAN IN PARIS, 1951

658 It's electrifyin'

Greaser John Travolta gets it on with the completely transformed Olivia Newton-John in her skintight outfit to the immortal strains of the classic pop number "You're the One I Want."

GREASE, 1978

659 Get aboard!

A washed-up hoofer (Fred Astaire) and a prima ballerina (Cyd Charisse) are unsure if they will be able to dance together until they hear an orchestra playing the haunting melody "Dancing in the Dark" in Central Park. They start to walk together in rhythm, then cautiously try a few dance steps, and soon we are presented with a stunning dance sequence that is the highlight of this wonderful movie.

THE BAND WAGON, 1953

660 One day to last them the rest of their lives

Homesick American singer Paul Allison meets fellow American Marcia Mornay at the May Day Fair. They spend the day enjoying each other's company—singing, dancing, walking, and swinging on a flower-decorated swing. He asks her if she has had fun, and she replies, "Fun. I never knew there was such fun…such, such happiness. I've never been so happy in my life. It's been wonderful."

MAYTIME, 1937

661 The songs…the romance… the music…the drama…the magic…

The best knight of the Round Table, Sir Lancelot, takes great interest in Guinevere, the queen of his best friend and noble leader, King Arthur.

Lancelot: "Dap, you are older than I. You know this earth better than I. I only fell upon it a few hours ago."

Dap: "What are you talking about?"

Lancelot: "Guinevere!"

CAMELOT, 1967

662 Truth beauty freedom love

After an unconscious Argentinian falls through his ceiling, aspiring writer Christian suddenly finds himself being convinced to write a new show for the Moulin Rouge by the great Parisian artist Toulouse Lautrec, who asks him if he believes in love.

Christian: "Love? Above all things I believe in love! Love is like oxygen! Love is a many-splendored thing! Love lifts us up where we belong! All you need is love!"

Toulouse Lautrec: "See? You can't fool us! You are the voice of the children of the revolution!"

MOULIN ROUGE! 2001

663 It's scrumdiddlyumptious!

Peanut-factory owner Mr. Salt has promised his spoiled daughter Veruca that he will find her one of the five golden tickets hidden in Wonka Bars so that she can win a tour of Willy Wonka's magical chocolate factory.

Mr. Salt: "For five days now, the entire flipping factory's been on the job. They haven't shelled a peanut in there since Monday. They've been shelling flavored chocolate bars from dawn till dusk!"

Veruca Salt: "Make them work nights!"

WILLY WONKA & THE CHOCOLATE FACTORY, 1971

664 We're off to see the wizard...

The Munchkins and Glinda the Good Witch show Dorothy the way she must take to reach the Wonderful Wizard of Oz in this delightful musical number. She must "Follow the yellow brick road...follow the yellow brick road...."

THE WIZARD OF OZ, 1939

665 Biggest musical under the sun!

Feisty Annie Oakley is an incredible shot. She explains to us in one memorable musical moment that she was raised, "Doin' What Comes Naturally."

ANNIE GET YOUR GUN, 1950

666 A medieval comedy of errors!

There is an air of intrigue and subterfuge at the royal court, where a ghastly murder plot is taking shape. Danny Kaye plays the jester, Hawkins, who must make sure that the poison reaches its target: "I've got it! I've got it! The pellet with the poison's in the vessel with the pestle; the chalice from the palace has the brew that is true! Right?"

THE COURT JESTER, 1956

667 Stayin' alive!

The Bee Gees's famous music strikes up at the 2001 Odyssey Disco. Young Brooklyn store clerk Tony Manero gets out onto the floor in a tight white suit and platform shoes, aims his arm to the sky, and magnificently struts his stuff.

SATURDAY NIGHT FEVER, 1977

668 You'll never want to leave

Once in a hundred years, and for one day only, the past opens up into the present in the Highlands of Scotland, and the village of Brigadoon appears. Two lost hunters from New York stumble into the past in a memorable scene that asks the audience to suspend its disbelief and enjoy the magic.

BRIGADOON, 1954

669 Anyone for coffee?

Ambitious Mick Travis is looking to climb the ladder of success. When Imperial Coffee's leading salesman dies, he uses his charm and enthusiasm to impress the manager and get the job. But before he's set free to find his fortune, Travis is handed over to Gloria Row for some coaching: "The future is in your hands, Mr. Travis. Take it…now!"

O LUCKY MAN! 1973

670 "We'll find a new way of living!"

After some remarkably energetic choreography, there's a scene reminiscent of Shakespeare's *Romeo and Juliet*. On a tenement fire escape, rather than a balcony, the two star-crossed lovers, Maria and Tony, sing together: "Tonight, tonight…"

WEST SIDE STORY, 1961

671 Naughty but nice!

Maurice Chevalier, with his wonderful French accent, breaks into his much imitated, but nevertheless enchanting prayer, "Thank Heaven for little girls, for little girls get bigger every day."

GIGI, 1958

672 And the winner is…

Norman arrives late at the Academy Awards ceremony, approaches the stage, and interrupts Vicki's thank-you speech: "Congratulations, my dear. I made it just in time, didn't I? May I borrow the end of your speech to make a speech of my own?" He then drunkenly pleads with the assembled Hollywood glitterati for a job.

A STAR IS BORN, 1954

673 Nothing's impossible!

Lucky pretends to be clumsy, graceless, and uncoordinated.
Watched by his dance instructor, he slips and slides around,
and ends up falling on the floor. Then he starts to sing:
"Nothing's impossible I have found,
When my chin is on the ground,
I pick myself up, dust myself off, start all over again."
SWING TIME, 1936

674 Ahead of his time

Local librarian Marian Paroo confronts con artist Harold Hill, who
has fallen in love with her, accusing him of lying about the
Conservatory of Music in Indiana that he claims to have attended.
She shows him a page torn from an Indiana journal that proves the
town was not even built until the year after he claims to have been
there. She tells him, "I was going to use it against you, but now
I give it to you with my love."
THE MUSIC MAN, 1962

675 It's supercalifragilisticexpialidocious!

This timeless favorite is full of magical fantasy moments, infectious songs ("Supercalifragilisticexpialidocious" being just one fine example), and memorable dance routines. In one such number, Cockney chimney sweep Bert (Dick Van Dyke) and his fellow sweeps perform a wonderful "Chimney Sweep Ballet," complete with sooty faces and chimney brushes, on the rooftops of London.

MARY POPPINS, 1964

676 "Damn it! I knew I should have gotten that spare tire fixed."

Brad Majors and Janet Weiss suffer a tire blowout during a storm, and Brad volunteers to go to a castle they passed a few miles back to get help, "Maybe they have a telephone…." Janet wants to go, too, and, as they step out of the vehicle into the rain, she places a newspaper over her head. Curiously, members of the audience in the cinema then do the same—this movie is famed for its audience participation. So why the newspapers? Because at this moment, the audience members pull out water pistols and begin shooting them into the air to simulate the rainstorm!

THE ROCKY HORROR PICTURE SHOW, 1975

677 Hollywood never faced a zanier Zero hour!

Crooked and broke, theatrical impresario Max Bialystock, and his accountant, Leo Bloom, plan to make money by producing a flop musical and skimming the proceeds. However, on the first night of their all-singing, all-dancing, Nazi musical, *Springtime for Hitler*, their surefire flop proves to be a huge hit with the audience and the critics. The producers are dumbfounded and Max wonders, "How could this happen? I was so careful. I picked the wrong play, the wrong director, the wrong cast. Where did I go right?"

THE PRODUCERS, 1968

678 Ben and Pardner shared everything—even their wife!

Ben and Pardner share everything in life, including the woman they bought from a Mormon to be their wife. They also discover a novel way of getting gold. They tunnel underneath a gold-rush boomtown to collect all the fallen gold dust that has slipped down through the cracks in the saloon floor!

PAINT YOUR WAGON, 1969

679 One of the most energetic musicals of all time!

The dynamic dancing and sensational acrobatics during the barn-raising scene easily take the Best Moment In This Movie award.

SEVEN BRIDES FOR SEVEN BROTHERS, 1954

680 "I don't want to go to war."

A group of soldiers board a train to go off to World War I, which is being presented as the "new attraction" at the Brighton Amusement Pier—complete with shooting gallery, a scoreboard of the dead, prizes 'n' all! They sing as they leave, "Good-byeee…good-byeeeee…"

OH! WHAT A LOVELY WAR, 1969

681 "Don't you know everyone wants to laugh?"

My personal favorite is watching Donald O'Connor do his zany dance routine for Gene Kelly and Debbie Reynolds. In this hilarious and amazingly acrobatic dance sequence, he seduces a dummy, runs up walls, does backflips and somersaults, runs into a brick wall, and crashes through a backdrop—and all just to "make 'em laugh!"

SINGIN' IN THE RAIN, 1952

682 **We're headin' for the Laughin' Place!**

Uncle Remus tries to cheer up little Johnny, who is upset over his parents' separation, with a tale and a song: "It happened on one o' them Zip-A-Dee-Doo-Dah days. Now that's the kind of day when you can't open yo' mouth without a song jumpin' right out of it!"

SONG OF THE SOUTH, 1946

683 **Come on, everybody, let's go on the town!**

The navy is in town and these three sailors are going to make the most of their leave! As they wander open-jawed through the city, Gabey, Chip, and Ozzie become so excited that they have to break into song: "New York, New York…" It's a wonderful town!

ON THE TOWN, 1949

684 **MGM's glorious love story with music**

Judy Garland joins a group of ladies in flowery hats and young people on a trolley car on a beautiful spring day. They suddenly and memorably burst into song: "Clang, clang, clang went the trolley…"

MEET ME IN ST. LOUIS, 1944

685 Arise... arise...

The cabaret star, her boyfriend, and her aristocratic lover are in a beer garden in Germany at the rise of Hitler's regime. A handsome, blond-haired, blue-eyed boy stands up to sing and is soon joined by a chorus of similarly clad fresh-faced Aryans. As the camera tilts to reveal the boy's brown uniform and swastika armband, the Hitler youths sing "Tomorrow Belongs to Me."

CABARET, 1972

686 "Etcetera etcetera etcetera"

There's a famous scene, full of pomp and circumstance, in which all of the King of Siam's children are presented—in a seemingly endless procession—to their new English teacher, Anna Leonowens.

THE KING AND I, 1956

687 "My mother thanks you, my father thanks you, my sister thanks you, and I thank you."

In the rousing finale of this biographic story, patriot George M. Cohan (James Cagney) gets in step with the troops and civilians as they march down Pennsylvania Avenue to his song, "Over There."

YANKEE DOODLE DANDY, 1942

688 The rehearsal

Gilbert and Sullivan suffer a stale creative period and begin to drift apart, but, after visiting an exhibition of Japanese culture that fuels their imaginations, they get together once more to produce *The Mikado*. In one lengthy scene in which Gilbert directs several singers, one tries out an accent, and Gilbert barks, "Again, please— this time in English!" Another actor tries out something, saying it amuses him. The icy Gilbert produces an assassin's grin, then bellows, "Yes, but does it amuse me?"

TOPSY-TURVY, 1999

689 Oh toot!

Crackpot inventor Dick Van Dyke and his children follow a candy baron through his factory in an attempt to sell him the idea for their unique sweet. It's "the fruit that you toot"—a musical lollipop called "Toot Sweets." The hard-nosed businessman tries one, and is surprisingly pleased. The sweets are passed around the staff, and a large musical number, filled with optimism and triumph, breaks out—until hundreds of dogs, lured by all the whistling, suddenly storm the factory floor!

CHITTY CHITTY BANG BANG, 1968

690 "Let it be me!"

Michael Douglas plays a director auditioning dancers for a large stage production. Many are eliminated, and things get tougher. The dancers are trying too hard to impress him but he's looking for something else: "Goddammit, now can't anybody up there hear me! Just let your hair down! Can't you talk? All of you, just talk, to me, to each other! Jesus Christ!"

A CHORUS LINE, 1985

691 Oh! Baby! What a show!

Chorus girl and understudy Peggy Sawyer is given a pep talk by her director just moments before she's due on stage, "…But you keep your feet on the ground and your head on those shoulders of yours and go out. And Sawyer, you're going out a youngster, but you've got to come back a star." Peggy is then pushed out onto the stage for her leading performance debut.

42ND STREET, 1933

692 Matchmaking madness

Widowed matchmaker Dolly Levi takes a trip to Yonkers, New York, to see "well-known unmarried half-a-millionaire" Horace Vandergelder.
Ticket seller: "Gonna marry him yourself, Dolly?"
Dolly: "Why, Mr. Sullivan, whatever put such a preposterous idea into my head…your head!"
HELLO, DOLLY! 1969

693 "Just keeps rolling along…"

There is a classic scene in which, amid an impressive montage sequence that climaxes with a thrilling panning shot around his head, Paul Robeson sings the immortal song "Ol' Man River."
SHOW BOAT, 1936

694 "If I could talk to the animals…"

World-renowned veterinarian Dr. Dolittle (Rex Harrison), who can speak many animal languages, is en route from Puddleby-by-the-Marsh to the South Seas to find the elusive Great Pink Sea Snail. He is introduced to the legendary Pushme-Pullyou, which is so incredible that it sends Albert Blossom (Richard Attenborough) into a frenzied song-and-dance routine to "I've Never Seen Anything Like It."
DOCTOR DOLITTLE, 1967

695 May your days be merry

In a truly magical finale, Bing Crosby and Danny Kaye successfully get their reunion show on stage for their old army general and are happily reunited with their girls. Then the merry group opens up the barn doors. Outside it's snowing. Everyone breaks into, "I'm dreaming of a white Christmas…"

WHITE CHRISTMAS, 1954

696 The one…the only…the original!

Nurse Ensign Nellie Forbush breaks into song while washing her hair on a beautiful beach: "I'm gonna wash that man right out of my hair…" In this case, the man is the French planter Emile De Becque.

SOUTH PACIFIC, 1958

697 If you can't be famous…be infamous!

Roxie Hart is up on a murder rap and she needs representation. Matron "Mama" Morton introduces her, for a price, to top legal man Billy Flynn. He charges $5000 for his "expertise," confidently declaring, "I don't mean to toot my own horn, but if Jesus Christ lived in Chicago today, and he had come to me and he had $5000, let's just say things would have turned out differently."

CHICAGO, 2002

698 King of the hoofers

Tom and Ellen Bowen are a brother-and-sister dance act booked to appear in London at the time of the royal wedding. In one wonderful scene, Fred Astaire as Tom dances on the walls and the ceiling of his hotel room. (The specially designed set actually rotated.)

ROYAL WEDDING, 1951

699 Her head is in the clouds

Shirley Temple plays a little girl who is doted on by a group of aviators—friends of her late father, who "cracked up and went to heaven." In one scene, her closest pal, "Loop" Merritt, arranges a birthday party for the child, at which she sings the famous song "On the Good Ship Lollipop" to all gathered around her.

BRIGHT EYES, 1934

700 The loverliest motion picture of them all!

Linguistics professor Henry Higgins takes his protégée Eliza Dolittle to Ascot, where she manages to convince everyone that she is a lady. The aristocrats are all suitably charmed and accept her little grammatical peculiarities as the fashionable "small talk" until the memorable climax when she shouts at the horse she has bet on, "Move yer bloomin' arse!"

MY FAIR LADY, 1964

Cinema
Greats

In an attempt to resist reiterating the same movies that keep turning up over and over again, I have sifted through my collection to extract a few great titles that are sometimes forgotten from "best movies" lists. These may not be the classics that everyone has seen, and they are not all critically acclaimed award winners, but each film presented here has made its mark and stuck in the minds of those who have seen it. Hopefully you will find some of your favorites in this chapter, but you will also be introduced to some little gems that you may have overlooked in the past.

Previous page: Robert Duvall and Marlon Brando in
The Godfather (1972).

701 False horizons

In one scene from this beautiful film, the entire village heads out to sea in their fishing boats at night to watch a great ocean liner pass by. What transpires is so mesmerizing, its image will live with you for the rest of your life.

AMARCORD, 1973

702 A suitable case for treatment

Morgan Delt is a delightfully eccentric man trying to prevent his ex-wife from remarrying. One of the most wonderful scenes is when Morgan goes to Highgate cemetery with his socialist mother to visit the grave of Karl Marx.

MORGAN! 1966

703 Thank God for color

The greatest moment in this movie has to be when Sean Thornton (John Wayne) follows Mary Kate (Maureen O'Hara) to the train station, then drags the beautiful flame-haired actress five miles across the lush green Irish countryside, followed by a growing crowd of spectators.

THE QUIET MAN, 1952

704 Women love him... and he can't help loving them back

This tale of a young man's (Albert Finney) racy adventures includes a notoriously lustful foreplay scene involving food and the pleasures of eating.

TOM JONES, 1963

705 When two cultures collide...it's electric!

Detective John Book (Harrison Ford) is in young Amish woman Rachel Lapp's (Kelly McGillis) barn, fixing his car. He manages to get the electrical system working and the radio starts playing "Wonderful World." He holds her in his arms, and they dance together in the light of the car's headlamps.

WITNESS, 1985

706 Mr. Right?

Charles (Hugh Grant) tells Fiona (Kristin Scott Thomas) that he is mad about the American girl (Andie MacDowell) who is marrying someone else. He asks Fiona if she has found her Mr. Right yet, and she reveals that she has been in love with someone for a long time. "Have you? Who is that, Fifi?" he asks. "You, Charlie," she replies.

FOUR WEDDINGS AND A FUNERAL, 1993

707 "I make no apologies for sounding egotistical—because I am!"

Headstrong country girl Sybylla Melvyn has great hopes for a future writing career when she leaves her dusty outback home to visit relatives in New South Wales. Her kind relatives take her in hand and give her a makeover, but the determined young girl knows that she has the brains to get what she wants in life:

Aunt Gussie: "Oh, fancy you're clever, do you?"
Sybylla: "I rather hope so. I'm done for if I'm not!"

MY BRILLIANT CAREER, 1979

708 Life is in their hands—death is on their minds!

During a murder trial, one of the jurors points out something that no one else has noticed—the elderly witness who gave evidence against the defendant had pinch marks on his nose from wearing glasses, but he wasn't wearing them in court. Could an old man who wears glasses really have seen what he claims to have witnessed?

12 ANGRY MEN, 1957

709 Sharpness is a state of mind

The meticulously choreographed fights in this movie are awe inspiring, but when the characters actually begin flying, it is time to sit back, suspend disbelief, and travel into a film less ordinary!

CROUCHING TIGER, HIDDEN DRAGON, 2000

710 It's all about men!

If you thought that men could fight dirty, check out the feisty brawl in this movie between Miriam and Sylvia, which culminates with a ferocious bite to the leg. After the fight, Crystal has the final, magnificent word: "There's a name for you ladies, but it isn't used in high society, outside of a kennel."

THE WOMEN, 1939

711 Meet the model son who's been good too long

College boy Joel Goodson (Tom Cruise) makes an unforgettable entrance when he slides across the floor wearing white socks, a pink shirt, and tight underwear, while dancing and lip-synching to Bob Seger's "Old Time Rock & Roll."

RISKY BUSINESS, 1983

712 No remorse

Things turn sour for garbage man Kit Carruthers and his 15-year-old girlfriend, Holly Sargis, when her father tries to stop them from seeing each other. Kit kills Mr. Sargis in a matter-of-fact way. Neither of the youths shows any remorse for their actions as they go off into the woods to set up house together.

BADLANDS, 1973

713 One-man army

In a battle scene to remember, Samson (Victor Mature)— a biblical forerunner to Rambo—manages to destroy the entire Philistine army armed only with the jawbone of an ass.

SAMSON AND DELILAH, 1949

714 He loved the American Dream. With a vengeance.

Tony Montana (Al Pacino) faces overwhelming odds when assassins raid his mansion, but he is ready for them. He pulls out his M16 assault rifle with a grenade launcher attached and screams, "Say hello to my little friend!"

SCARFACE, 1983

715 What a glorious feeling!

Gene Kelly performs the screen's most famous dance routine in this classic movie—an unforgettable, joy-filled, lovestruck dance in a downpour, watched by a bemused policeman, while singing, "I'm singin' in the rain, just singin' in the rain what a glorious feeling, I'm happy again…"

SINGIN' IN THE RAIN, 1952

716 It's curtains for Nottingham

In one amazing acrobatic stunt, Robin Hood (Douglas Fairbanks) stabs the point of his dagger into a 40-foot curtain and rides all the way down it from the balcony to floor level.

ROBIN HOOD, 1922

717 Looks aren't everything!

Fireman Charlie "C. D." Bales—a modern-day Cyrano de Bergerac—responds wittily to a bully in a bar by challenging him to come up with a more imaginative insult for his big nose: "Obvious: Excuse me, is that your nose or did a bus park on your face?…Humorous: Laugh and the world laughs with you; sneeze and it's goodbye, Seattle."

ROXANNE, 1987

718 The man with the silver tongue meets the man with the Midas touch

In this, the quintessential James Bond movie, Goldfinger has 007 strapped spread-eagle to a table while an industrial laser cuts its way through the metal surface toward his manhood. James Bond lets his enemy know that interrogation won't work on him: "You've made your point, Goldfinger. Do you expect me to talk?" But that isn't what Goldfinger has in mind. "No, Mr. Bond," he replies, "I expect you to die."

GOLDFINGER, 1964

719 A side order of hilarity!

In a crowded New York restaurant, Sally (Meg Ryan) proves to Harry (Billy Crystal) that women can convincingly fake their orgasms—by simulating one right then and there! This great comic moment is then trumped by a woman at the next table, who tells the waiter, "I'll have what she's having."

WHEN HARRY MET SALLY, 1989

720 The chauffeur's daughter who learned her stuff in Paris!

Sabrina Fairchild (Audrey Hepburn) returns from Paris as a beautiful and refined young woman, and is given a ride home from the station by wealthy playboy David Larrabee (William Holden). He doesn't recognize her as the chauffeur's daughter, and asks her where she's been all his life, to which she charmingly replies, "Right over the garage."

SABRINA, 1954

721 The horror is driving him crazy

Jack Torrance has flipped out, and he's chasing his wife and son around the deserted snowbound hotel that he is managing for the winter. He corners his wife, Wendy, in the bathroom and begins to demolish the door with an ax as she stands, terrified, on the other side. He knocks through a panel in the door, crams his wild face into the small opening, and announces, "Heeeeeeeere's Johnny!"

THE SHINING, 1980

722 You can never go fast enough...

James Taylor does an excellent job as the obsessed driver in this strange road movie. In the final moments of the movie, the film freeze-frames and then catches fire as though in a projector.

TWO-LANE BLACKTOP, 1971

723 Love is in the hair

Four simple words had viewers of this comic movie howling with laughter, as Cameron Diaz's character, Mary, asks Ben Stiller's Ted, "Is that hair gel?"

THERE'S SOMETHING ABOUT MARY, 1998

724 Putting all their eggs in one basket

In one hilarious and chaotic scene in this riotous film, Groucho Marx is visited in his tiny ship's cabin by one person after another—everyone, it seems, wants to get into that little room. Margaret Dumont eventually puts us out of our misery by opening the door, causing everyone inside to pour out.

A NIGHT AT THE OPERA, 1935

725 The word is mightier that the sword

Ambitious valet-turned-spy Ulysses Diello invites destitute Countess Anna Staviska to become a conspirator in his secret "enterprise," and, in a slick verbal duel, they search for one another's weaknesses.

5 FINGERS, 1952

726 Water under the bridge

As Stan and Ollie discuss the fact that they delivered a deed to a valuable gold mine to the wrong woman, Stan remembers another of their hilarious blunders: "That's the first mistake we've made since that guy sold us the Brooklyn Bridge."

WAY OUT WEST, 1937

727 "Better to be king for a night than a schmuck for a lifetime."

Aspiring comedian Rupert Pupkin (Robert De Niro) compiles a cassette tape for comedy star Jerry Langford (Jerry Lewis) in his studio basement, while being constantly interrupted by his mother's nagging voice from upstairs.

THE KING OF COMEDY, 1983

728 "Here's one rap you ain't gonna beat!"

Gangster Eddie Bartlett (James Cagney) dies in the snow on the steps of a church in the arms of Panama Smith (Gladys George). A cop asks her, "Who is he?" and Panama simply replies, "He used to be a big shot."

THE ROARING TWENTIES, 1939

729 True confession

At a cathedral in San Salvador, sleazy American journalist Richard Boyle seeks forgiveness from a priest, who tells him he must change his ways. But Boyle knows "that's gonna be a little tough."

SALVADOR, 1986

730 Cold comfort

There are several steamy moments between Jackie Shawn (Julie Christie) and her hairdresser, George Roundy (Warren Beatty), in this movie. One that springs to mind is when the couple sneaks away from a party to a darkened kitchen. Minutes later, the refrigerator door slowly opens to illuminate them in the act.

SHAMPOO, 1975

731 An opera star. A Mountie. The Canadian Rockies.

In a beautiful celebrated duet, Sergeant Bruce (Nelson Eddy) and Marie de Flor (Jeanette MacDonald) sing "Indian Love Call" in front of the scenic backdrop of the Canadian Rockies.

ROSE-MARIE, 1936

732 Everyone plays a part

Just as dinner is being served, a curtain opens and a group of friends suddenly find themselves on a stage playing to an audience. Henri Senechal's eyes open wide with stage fright as he exclaims, "I don't know my lines."

THE DISCREET CHARM OF THE BOURGEOISIE, 1972

733 You are cordially invited to George and Martha's for an evening of fun and games

Elizabeth Taylor performs wonderfully as Martha throughout this movie, particularly in the scene in which George (Richard Burton) holds a gun to the back of her head while she tells their guests about an embarrassing incident from his past.

WHO'S AFRAID OF VIRGINIA WOOLF? 1966

734 Dance she did, and dance she must

Beautiful young dancer Victoria Page is interviewed by Boris Lermontov for a position with his prestigious ballet company:

Boris: "Why do you want to dance?"
Victoria: "Why do you want to live?"
Boris: "Well, I don't know exactly why, er, but I must."
Victoria: "That's my answer, too."

THE RED SHOES, 1948

735 She was the first

Against a background of eerie calm, skipper Robert Shaw recalls the sinking of the USS *Indianapolis* in 1945, holding his fellow shark hunters absolutely spellbound. With his eyes glazed and distant, he describes the accident in shark-infested waters that claimed hundreds of lives—just the sort of story you want to hear when you're being stalked by a great white shark!

JAWS, 1975

736 Heat wave

This is the movie in which Marilyn Monroe (as The Girl) makes her world-famous pose on top of a New York subway grating—her beautiful white dress billows up around her knees as a train passing underground sends up a cool breeze.

The Girl: "Isn't it delicious?"
Richard Sherman: "Sort of cools the ankles, doesn't it?"

THE SEVEN YEAR ITCH, 1955

737 "When the ruthless ambitions of a man threaten to engulf the world..."

This is the film to bathe in if action-filled, swashbuckling sea battles are your thing. Captain Geoffrey Thorpe sets out, with the Queen's blessing, to thwart Spain's plans for world domination, but there is a traitor at court—Lord Wolfingham. In the climactic scene, we are treated to one of the best duels ever screened, as Thorpe takes on the traitor, accompanied by a thrilling musical score by Erich Wolfgang Korngold.

THE SEA HAWK, 1940

738 They're young... they're in love... and they kill people.

Dubbed the Ballet of Death, the amazingly edited finale of this Depression-era crime movie shows the last bloody stand of the young outlaws, who are ambushed in their car and riddled with bullets.

BONNIE AND CLYDE, 1967

739 Lt. Col. Frank Slade has a very special plan for the weekend...

In one hair-raising scene, blind Frank Slade (Al Pacino) takes a Ferrari for a test-drive, while his young companion, Charlie Simms (Chris O'Donnell), shouts directions to keep them from crashing.

SCENT OF A WOMAN, 1992

740 The bases are loaded...

Charlie finds his autistic brother's obsessive reciting of the Abbott and Costello "Who's on First?" wordplay routine incredibly frustrating: "Ray, you're never gonna solve it. It's not a riddle, because Who is on first base. That's a joke, Ray, it's comedy! But when *you* do it you're not funny. You're like the comedy of Abbott and Abbott!"

RAIN MAN, 19888

741 An offer he can't refuse

As movie mogul Jack Woltz wakes up in his Bel Air mansion, he notices something strange on the silk sheets beside him. It's blood—a lot of blood! He throws back the sheets to reveal a shocking sight—the butchered head of his priceless stallion, Khartoum.

THE GODFATHER, 1972

742 "You make love without fading out?"

There is a wonderful scene in which Tom Baxter, the fictional hero of the film *The Purple Rose of Cairo* steps out of the movie screen and speaks to Cecilia in the audience. There are, however, some drawbacks to the new man in her life: "I just met a wonderful new man. He's fictional, but you can't have everything."

THE PURPLE ROSE OF CAIRO, 1985

743 Once upon a time...

This wonderful film stars Jean Harlow as the sexy Vantine Jefferson and Clark Gable as Dennis Carson. My favorite is the final scene, in which Vantine helps Carson recuperate from a gunshot wound by reading him a children's bedtime story as he moves his hand up her leg!

RED DUST, 1932

744 Marilyn Monroe and her bosom companions

The two runaway musicians in drag see the band's voluptuous ukelele-playing singer, Sugar Kane (Marilyn Monroe), moving down the train platform, avoiding a jet of hot steam.

Jerry: "Look at that! Look how she moves. That's just like Jell-O on springs. She must have some sort of built-in motors. I tell you, it's a whole different sex!"

Joe: "What are you afraid of? Nobody's asking you to have a baby."

SOME LIKE IT HOT, 1959

745 Ride 'em, cowboy!

As the two mightiest nations on Earth try, via the telephone, to defuse an accidental nuclear attack, B52 pilot Major T. J. "King" Kong mounts his atom bomb as though it were a bucking bronco. He rides it cowboy-style toward its target with Stetson hat in hand, yelling "Yahoo!"

DR. STRANGELOVE, OR: HOW I LEARNED TO STOP WORRYING AND LOVE THE BOMB, 1964

746 When a plan goes awry

Texan bar owner Julien Marty suspects his wife Abby of being unfaithful with his bartender Ray. He hires a sleazy private eye to kill them, and that's where everything starts to come undone:

Marty: "I got a job for you."

Private Detective: "Uh, well, if the pay's right, and it's legal, I'll do it."

Marty: "It's not strictly legal."

Private Detective: "Well, if the pay's right, I'll do it."

BLOOD SIMPLE, 1984

747 Amateur thief

Reformed jewel thief John Robie meets H. H. Hughson, a Lloyds of London insurance agent, for lunch to discuss a theft:

Robie: "You're given an expense allowance to pay for all the meals you eat on the job. Right? But this meal is free. Now, are you going to deduct the price of a lunch from your expense account? Well, of course you're not. It would be stupid. Do you agree?"

Hughson: "Yes."

Robie: "You're a thief. Only an amateur thief, of course, but it will help you to sympathize with us professionals."

TO CATCH A THIEF, 1955

748 Who was he... What was his strange power?

Aristocrat Sir Percy Blakeney, the Scarlet Pimpernel, frequently recites the comical poem: "They seek him here. They seek him there. Those Frenchies seek him everywhere. Is he in Heaven? Is he in Hell? That damned elusive Pimpernel."

THE SCARLET PIMPERNEL, 1934

749 You're not safe anywhere

Hunted advertising executive Roger O. Thornhill (Cary Grant) finds himself alone in the middle of a bleak prairie landscape. A biplane drones into view. As it gets closer and closer, a terrified Thornhill takes cover in a cornfield, but the plane is a crop-duster and thick clouds of poison start to fall from the sky.

NORTH BY NORTHWEST, 1959

750 Making up for lost time

In the final beach scene, a past secret is revealed to Baby Jane Hudson and she replies, "You mean, all this time we could have been friends?" She then buys two strawberry ice creams and spins and dances around on the sand.

WHAT EVER HAPPENED TO BABY JANE? 1962

World
Cinema

World cinema, foreign films, international movies—whatever term we use, it serves to confirm that Hollywood is not the only influence on the future of cinema, and that other countries are more than capable of entertaining the globe's masses. The films here are only the tip of the iceberg; so many wonderful films could be included, but this little taster will have to suffice. Hopefully, it will inspire you to explore movies, perhaps previously neglected, from Europe, Mexico, Russia, Japan, and many other countries. Don't let subtitles dissuade you, and remember: popcorn tastes good in any language!

Previous page: Jean Seberg in *Breathless* (1960).

352

751 How did you spend your day, dear?

Catherine Deneuve plays a housewife who secretly becomes a prostitute to satisfy the sexual fantasies that she cannot fulfill with her husband. In one scene, one of her clients asks her to lie inside a coffin, to recreate his fantasy of mourning for a daughter, and we watch as the coffin starts to shake.

BELLE DE JOUR, 1967

752 Oh, what a picture!

Feisty, young Amélie has stolen her widowed father's garden gnome as part of a plan to get him to travel, but she misses the last train, and she has to sleep in a photo booth, cuddled up with the strange, little creature.

AMÉLIE, 2001

753 First class delivery

A postman delivering mail to a small island near Naples, falls for the beautiful niece of the innkeeper over a game of bar football— she places the little white ball in her mouth and spits it out contemptuously when he makes a hesitant move towards her.

IL POSTINO, 1994

754 "Oooookay!"

Transported through time to the twentieth century with his peasant manservant, medieval prince Godefroy de Papincourt (Jean Reno) attacks a car with his sword, thinking it is a demon or a dragon.

LES VISITEURS, 1993

755 New heights

American socialite Irene Girard (Ingrid Bergman) and her pet arrive at her building in Rome, in a rush to prepare for the arrival of her dinner guests. Irene is headed off by the concierge, who informs her that, once again, the elevator is out of order.

EUROPA '51, 1951

756 Horrifying

This movie climaxes with a massacre on the Odessa steps—shots ring out, troops fire on civilians, and terrified people flee down the stairs. One woman is gunned down while cradling the body of her dead son. Then a young mother is hit, and her baby carriage tumbles out of control down the steep steps.

BATTLESHIP POTEMKIN, 1925

757 Indelible images

The shocking and disturbing opening sequence of Luis Buñuel's surreal film, which shows a man slicing a woman's wide-open eye in half with a sharp-edged razor, sticks in the mind as much as the image of ants coming out of a hole in a man's hand.

UN CHIEN ANDALOU, 1929

758 Spokesman of the people

Gérard Depardieu gives such a magnificent defense of his country, his beliefs, and himself in court that he nearly dies of exhaustion, and he loses his voice entirely.

DANTON, 1983

759 The nightmare world of a virgin's dreams becomes the screen's shocking reality!

Carole Ledoux is mentally frail. When her sister leaves her alone in their apartment to go on a vacation, Carole's fear of solitude causes her to have kaleidoscopic nightmares. She believes she is being attacked—that hands are coming at her, out of the walls!

REPULSION, 1965

760 Silent witness

Introverted theater mime Baptiste Debureau (played by mime artist Jean-Louis Barrault) reveals, through a remarkable mime, that a missing watch was stolen by a man, and he proves that raven-haired beauty Garance is not the pickpocket.

LES ENFANTS DU PARADIS, 1945

761 The mighty warriors who became the seven national heroes of a small town

Poor Japanese villagers who are being threatened by a gang of bandits seek the advice of an elder named Gisaku, who recommends that they "find hungry samurai" who will fight to protect their village in return for only food and shelter.

SEVEN SAMURAI, 1954

762 A change in direction

Wealthy fashion designer Petra von Kant makes it clear to her friend Sidonie von Grasenab that she has no use for men. When Sidonie introduces her to beautiful 23-year-old Karin Thimm, who wants to be a model, Petra instantly falls for her.

THE BITTER TEARS OF PETRA VON KANT, 1972

763 Made to measure

A young student enters a clothing boutique, run by three beautiful and mysterious girls, to buy a suit for the public reading of his newly published book. One revealingly dressed girl assists him in front of the mirror, seductively adjusting his lapels, fastening his buttons, and making rather encouraging noises!

THREE WOMEN IN LOVE, 1989

764 Freeze-frame

In one scene, there is an epic battle on the frozen Lake Peipus between the invading Teutonic Knights and the Russian army, accompanied by Prokofiev's magnificent score.

ALEXANDER NEVSKY, 1938

765 Death is not a personal journey

Alexandre, who is terminally ill, stands in the pharmacy, waiting for the chemist to fill his prescription. Outside, he sees a young Albanian windshield cleaner being abducted into a van. Alexandre goes to his rescue, resolving to get the poor boy back to his war-torn homeland.

ETERNITY AND A DAY, 1998

766 A triumph—what a nose!

Aging and mortally wounded, Cyrano de Bergerac visits his true love at the convent one last time. He baits a nun there by telling her that he ate meat that day even though it is a Friday, then he gives us a most poetic end.

CYRANO DE BERGERAC, 1990

767 "I have a strange feeling… I'm not alone in the world."

Polish singer Weronika feels she is not alone in the world, while in France, music teacher Véronique has similar feelings. Unbeknownst to them, the women are identical in appearance and they share the same talents. One day, while flicking through photos from a school trip to Krakow, Véronique finds a picture of her life double.

THE DOUBLE LIFE OF VÉRONIQUE, 1991

768 Nuremberg 1828

Devoid of all educational and social skills, and suddenly cast out into the streets, Kaspar Hauser stands awestruck in the square, incapable of making any decision and grasping a mysterious note.

THE MYSTERY OF KASPAR HAUSER, 1974

769 Saved by the idea of death

The severity of nature is impressively captured in this movie during Captain Vladimir Arseniev and Dersu Uzala's expedition to a frozen Siberian lake. When a windstorm suddenly emerges and covers their tracks they become lost, but Dersu takes charge and frantically cuts long grass to form a shelter and save their lives.

DERSU UZALA, 1975

770 Odd methods

Four thieves devise an ingenious plan to rob a jewelry store in Paris. However, despite their skill and confidence, they get into difficulties during the robbery as they try to gain access to the jewels using a variety of unusual tools, including a fire extinguisher and an umbrella.

RIFIFI, 1954

771 Only have eyes for you

Christina Delasalle finds her husband's missing corpse in the bathtub, his blank, white eyes wide open. Suddenly, the body rises from the bath and reaches out toward her—Christina drops dead with fright. The corpse then removes the "blind" contact lenses from his eyes, goes to the door, and kisses his mistress.

LES DIABOLIQUES, 1955

772 You cannot choose your relatives

Despairing concert musician Charles Aznavour has taken refuge as a pianist in a bar in Paris. His brother turns up at the bar, pursued by criminals, and there's a confrontation. The bar's musical trio keeps playing through it all, and the barman joins them to sing a song about "Framboise."

SHOOT THE PIANIST, 1960

773 Give peas a chance

Woyzeck is a soldier, living on an experimental diet of peas, whose mind is becoming unhinged as he struggles to support his child and its mother. In one poignant scene, he shaves his superior officer with a very sharp razor while being lectured on decency.

WOYZECK, 1978

774 Jolly boating weather

When Fitzcarraldo's paddle steamer is boarded by Amazonian tribesmen, he plays them an opera record on his wind-up gramophone as they watch, mesmerized.

FITZCARRALDO, 1982

775 The spirit of cinema

The projectionist tilts a mirror next to the projector to capture the image that is being screened in the cinema. He plays it across the projection room, and then lets it loose through the window to cover the wall of a building in the square, where villagers can watch free of charge.

CINEMA PARADISO, 1989

776 Bleak and compelling

Two men are guided into the Zone by the Stalker to find the Room, where one's secret hopes come true. They complete their journey on a small, open rail gurney uncertain of what to expect.

STALKER, 1979

777 "You live and you suffer."

In postwar Italy, jobs are scarce, so Antonio Ricci is overjoyed when he manages to get one. A means of transport is essential to the job, so he retrieves his bicycle from the pawnbrokers. When the bike gets stolen on his very first day, Antonio embarks on a journey with his small son to find the thief.

THE BICYCLE THIEF, 1948

778 No sweat

On his first day at a new school in Marseilles, dedicated teacher Joseph Pagnol faces a large class of boys, and he is nervous about winning their confidence. He momentarily rests his head on the blackboard, then sees the damp patch left on it by his nervous perspiration. He quickly rubs it off and turns to face the class again.

LA GLOIRE DE MON PERE, 1990

779 Just desserts

One of four gastronomes who come together for a final magnificent feast is discovered frozen to death in the garden in the open-topped Bugatti that he had so lovingly restored.

LA GRANDE BOUFFE, 1973

780 He's convinced he is to blame

Young Archibaldo is given a music box to play with while his parents go out for the evening. His governess tells him that it has magical powers, and that a king once used it to rid himself of his enemies. As the boy winds the music box, a stray bullet from a fight outside smashes through the window and kills the governess.

THE CRIMINAL LIFE OF ARCHIBALDO DE LA CRUZ, 1955

781 A smorgasbord!

When the guests arrive at the home of the Sénéchals a day early for a dinner party, it is only the first in a series of bizarre obstacles that stop the bourgeois friends from dining together. In one humorous scene, they are even interrupted by a company of soldiers on maneuvers.

THE DISCREET CHARM OF THE BOURGEOISIE, 1972

782 Priceless black comedy

Two comrades are driven home in a carriage at the end of a night of revelry. They are closely pursued by a brass band, who play on the run while trying to catch the fistfuls of money being thrown to them.

UNDERGROUND, 1995

783 Not a drop to drink

Dastardly César Soubeyran (Yves Montand), hoping to drive Jean de Florette (Gérard Depardieu) and his family away from their newly inherited property, blocks off their water supply, little knowing the extent to which they will go to obtain water.

JEAN DE FLORETTE, 1986

784 Here's looking at you

Young thug Michel Poiccard (Jean-Paul Belmondo) pauses outside a movie theater and looks at his reflection as he gazes at a poster for a film starring Humphrey Bogart. He reverently whispers, "Bogey," then imitates his hero, blowing wispy smoke from his cigarette and running his thumb across his lower lip.

BREATHLESS, 1960

785 Dead ringer

Tom Ripley (Alain Delon) assumes the identity of a rich playboy, then makes a move on his girl. Their bodies get close together, she hesitates, we see their eyes in close-up—his, sinister, hers, wide and appealing—and, just as their lips are about to meet, he grabs a guitar, places it in her hands, and commands her to play.

PLEIN SOLEIL, 1959

786 Music was his passion. Survival was his masterpiece.

The soulful piano music of Chopin's *Nocturne in C* played by Wladyslaw Szpilman (Adrien Brody) in a hollowed-out apartment in the midst of desolation, lends a bizarre beauty to an unfathomable night.

THE PIANIST, 2002

787 There are angels on the streets of Berlin

Damiel, an angel watching over Berlin, observes a circus rehearsal and he is immediately captivated by a French trapeze artist named Marion who is practicing her act while wearing an angel costume.

WINGS OF DESIRE, 1987

788 Until death us do part

Maria Braun's married life lasts only a day and a half before her husband disappears. When her brother-in-law returns from the war, he comes to the American bar where she works with the news that her husband is dead. In shock, she asks a young soldier named Bill to dance with her.

THE MARRIAGE OF MARIA BRAUN, 1979

789 "Curst greed of gold, what crimes thy tyrant power has caused."

The movie opens on the breathtaking landscape of the Amazonian mountainside in the heart of the jungle. Tiny figures of men can be seen descending the steepest imaginable trail. They disappear over the horizon, then reappear in the foreground on the next mountain— it is the expedition of Gonzalo Pizarro searching for El Dorado.

AGUIRRE, THE WRATH OF GOD, 1972

790 Memory lane

A professor in his twilight years goes on a road trip to a ceremony honoring his life's work. When he picks up a spirited young woman and her two boyfriends on the road, he is compelled to reflect on his life, and to remember his more youthful days.

WILD STRAWBERRIES, 1957

791 Read it and weep

Catherine Lelievre employs a new maid named Sophie, who comes with excellent references, but also with a secret that is not let out of the bag until one day, when she is left a note on the kitchen table.

LA CÉRÉMONIE, 1995

792 That waggle dance

A festively decorated dining table adorned with rose petals stands abandoned in the center of a courtyard in the rain. Then we hear the voice of Marcello Mastroianni describing the movements of bees and the queen bee's dance.

THE BEEKEEPER, 1986

793 A feast for the senses

The guests at Babette's feast vow not to comment upon the exquisite banquet, believing it to be a test of their beliefs. However, Lorenz Lowenhielm, a visiting old general, is in a state of ecstasy over the wonderful food. He cannot stop talking about it, despite the many amusing attempts of the other guests to change the subject.

BABETTE'S FEAST, 1987

794 "The first thing God created was the journey; then came doubt, and nostalgia."

A group of people, including Harvey Keitel as a movie director searching for rare Greek film footage, take advantage of the thick fog and go outside for a walk—it's the only safe time to avoid the snipers. Keitel, who has fallen behind in the fog, hears a car screech up, followed by screams and shots. He rushes after his friends, only to discover their bodies—his reaction is heart-wrenching.

ULYSSES' GAZE, 1995

795 Amen

Wealthy Fabregard takes advantage of the newly arrived, ailing parish priest to strike a bargain over the funeral arrangements for his dear departed wife.

THE DIARY OF A COUNTRY PRIEST, 1950

796 When the time is right

French resistance officer Lieutenant Fontaine calmly awaits his chance to escape from the vehicle in which he is being taken to prison. He reaches for the door handle, pauses, then tries again. He finally seizes his chance as the vehicle slows at a train crossing, but he is swiftly caught and beaten by the German soliders.

A MAN ESCAPED, 1956

797 Mass appeal

Jean-Louis, a devout young Catholic, notices a girl named Françoise in the crowd at Sunday Mass and decides to marry her. She slips away before they can meet, but he is determined to remain faithful to his chosen bride until they do meet. However, a short time later he is stranded by a blizzard, and must spend the night with the beautiful Maud.

MY NIGHT AT MAUD'S, 1969

798 We all have something we want

During the opening scenes of this Luis Buñuel classic, wealthy businessman Fernando Rey is getting ready for a journey, but before he leaves he orders his valet to burn everything that is associated with a certain woman.

THAT OBSCURE OBJECT OF DESIRE, 1977

799 Living on his wits

In postwar Germany, 12-year-old Edmund is chased away from his job of digging graves for having no work permit. On the way home, he collects coal that falls from a truck, and he watches a crowd of people gathering around a dead horse in the street, seeking its flesh.

GERMANY YEAR ZERO, 1947

800 Survival, regret, loss, and reconstruction

A Parisian actress and a Japanese architect are kindred spirits united by guilt—by their shame at being survivors. They emerge from a hotel, the New Hiroshima, after their lovers' tryst, forever altered.

HIROSHIMA MON AMOUR, 1959

Epics

What makes an epic film? These movies are often exquisite and beautifully composed masterpieces that focus on historical events, legendary figures, or great achievements. They may center on a heroic quest, an epic adventure, a remarkable romance, or the life of a famous swashbuckling character; or they may serve to bring a classic text to life, including the Bible, the Mahabharata, or the works of William Shakespeare. These lavish spectacles fill the screen and our imaginations while recreating momentous events from our history and mythology, to entertain each new generation that encounters them.

Previous page: Peter O'Toole and Anthony Quinn in *Lawrence of Arabia* (1962).

801 In memory, love lives forever.

In one mesmerizing scene, a young Indian officer (Naveen Andrews) seats the nurse (Juliette Binoche) in a rope-and-pulley sling, places a flaming torch in her hand, and hoists her upward to see the beautiful frescoes on the church ceiling.

THE ENGLISH PATIENT, 1996

802 "God opens the sea with a blast of His nostrils!"

This biblical epic includes the legendary scene of the miraculous parting of the Red Sea—Moses holds his staff up to the sky and utters, "The Lord of Hosts will do battle for us. Behold his mighty hand." The sea parts into two great walls of swirling water, and Moses leads his people safely through to the other side before the water comes crashing down on the Egyptians pursuing them.

THE TEN COMMANDMENTS, 1956

803 "Sire, we need more heirs."

Oscar-winning actor Charles Laughton, as the notorious King Henry VIII, reluctantly beds his fourth wife, Anne of Cleves (Elsa Lanchester), with his famous sigh: "The things I've done for England."

THE PRIVATE LIFE OF HENRY VIII, 1933

804 The man of violence in whose place Christ died

Anthony Quinn plays the murderous thief Barabbas, who was spared from crucifixion instead of Jesus—something that haunts him for the rest of his life. One spine-chilling moment that occurs during the crucifixion scene is a solar eclipse and shooting was even delayed so that they could catch this genuine phenomenon on film.

BARABBAS, 1962

805 Smooth talker

Rose DeWitt Bukater climbs over the rail of the huge ship in her elegant evening gown and is about to throw herself into the sea when young Irishman Jack Dawson arrives and takes an unusual approach to stop her: "I'm not looking forward to jumping in after you. But like I said, I don't see a choice. I guess I'm kind of hoping you'll come back over the rail and get me off the hook here."

TITANIC, 1997

806 "The delicious debauchery!"

The empress Poppaea (Claudette Colbert) is bathing in a large tub of ass's milk, and she calls out to her handmaiden, "Take off your clothes and get in here!"

SIGN OF THE CROSS, 1932

807 His triumph changed the world forever

Having taken up the cause of Indian independence, Gandhi is faced with armed resistance by the British government. He adopts a policy of passive resistance, and endeavors to win freedom for his people without resorting to bloodshed: "Whenever I despair, I remember that the way of truth and love has always won. There may be tyrants and murderers, and, for a time, they may seem invincible, but in the end, they always fail."

GANDHI, 1982

808 He was the Lord of Ten Thousand Years, the absolute monarch of China. He was born to rule a world of ancient tradition. Nothing prepared him for our world of change.

In the Forbidden City, the little emperor Pu Yi leaps from his throne and comes running through a vast sea of sparkling cloth. As he breaks into the daylight at the top of a giant staircase, we see an incredible sight outside—his huge army of attendants, including 1500 eunuchs, is assembled to honor him.

THE LAST EMPEROR, 1987

809 The excesses of youth

The pillow fights and snowball battles of Napoleon's childhood shown at the beginning of this movie are choreographed on an epic scale as grand as any military battle captured on screen.

NAPOLEON, 1927

810 All good things must come to an end

Queen Elizabeth (Bette Davis) intended to marry the Earl of Essex (Errol Flynn) and give up her throne, but when she realizes that his plans would prove disastrous for England, she signs his death warrant. Moments before he leaves to face the executioner, Elizabeth begs Essex to ask for a pardon, but he refuses her mercy and goes to meet his doom.

THE PRIVATE LIVES OF ELIZABETH AND ESSEX, 1939

811 Where there's smoke, there's fire

The debauched emperor Nero (Peter Ustinov) sits, playing his lyre and taking great pleasure in watching Rome burn down. The fires are part of his own scheme to blame the Christians for destroying the city, which he plans to rebuild in his own image.

QUO VADIS? 1951

812 The life of Jesus Christ

This epic features a wealth of Hollywood stars in quite unexpected roles, but the scene that everyone remembers is that of John Wayne, as a centurion, stepping forward at Jesus' crucifixion to drawl out the line, "Truly, this man was the Son of God."

THE GREATEST STORY EVER TOLD, 1965

813 Back to nature

This romantic epic offers one wonderful scene in which the young men invite the vicar to join them in bathing naked in a woodland pond, which he does. Their innocent sport turns into a naked game of chase on the banks of the pond at exactly the moment that the film's matriarch, Mrs. Honeychurch, and her daughter, Lucy, arrive.

A ROOM WITH A VIEW, 1985

814 To have and to hold

William Wallace wishes only to farm his crops and to live in peace with his family. In a beautiful and touching scene, he marries his childhood sweetheart in secret, to prevent the English lord from exercising his right to *prima noctae* (bedding the bride on her wedding night), and, for a moment at least, everything seems perfect.

BRAVEHEART, 1995

815 The world's most honored motion picture

This epic is crammed with great moments, but the most memorable is the chariot race between Ben-Hur and the villainous Messala, who tries to kill Ben-Hur with his chariot's rotating blades. Unfortunately for Messala, his wheels lock, and his chariot is splintered into pieces. He is dragged along by his team of horses, then trampled into the ground by other horses.

BEN-HUR, 1959

816 "My Elizabeth shall be queen! And my blood will have been well spent!"

Richard Burton, as England's King Henry VIII, has his wife Anne Boleyn (Geneviève Bujold) charged with adultery when she fails to provide him a male heir. She refuses to divorce him, ensuring that her daughter, Elizabeth, remains heir to the throne, and she is sentenced to death. As Anne is led away to be beheaded, Henry sits alone in Windsor Castle, disconsolate and filled with remorse.

ANNE OF A THOUSAND DAYS, 1969

817 The Grand Hotel. Always the same. People come. People go…nothing ever happens.

In one memorable scene, lonely and depressed ballerina Grusinskaya (Greta Garbo) tries to get Baron Felix von Geigern (John Barrymore) to leave her hotel room. He confesses his love for her, but she insists that he must go saying, "I want to be alone."

GRAND HOTEL, 1932

818 Christmas at court

Henry II holds Christmas court at Chignon and commands his three sons, Richard (Lionheart), Geoffrey, and John to attend. John, despite being his father's favorite son, is rather prone to self-pity. He sits on a pile of straw, saying, "Poor John. Who says poor John? Don't everybody sob at once! My God! If I went up in flames there's not a living soul who'd piss on me to put the fire out!" To which Richard responds, "Let's strike a flint and see."

THE LION IN WINTER, 1968

819 Not so terrible

Of particular interest in Sergei Eisenstein's epic chronicles of the life of the infamous czar are the rich, operatic score by Sergei Prokofiev and the lavish banquet dance scene, which was shot in color, while the rest of the film was shot in black and white.

IVAN THE TERRIBLE, PART TWO, 1958

820 The reigning beauty of the screen!

This masterpiece is crammed with romantic moments played against grand, swirling musical motifs. Catherine the Great is played imaginatively by Marlene Dietrich, who in one scene holds gauze net over her face before allowing Count Alexei to kiss her.

THE SCARLET EMPRESS, 1934

821 When it rains on the poor, it really rains.

There is a knock at the large front door, and Leonard Bast (Samuel West) stands awkwardly as he tries to explain that he followed Helen Schlegel (Helena Bonham Carter) home because she inadvertently walked off with his umbrella—a common occurrence, it seems, judging by the collection by the door! The young man is not of her social class, but a connection has been made, and they are destined to meet again...

HOWARDS END, 1992

822 The true story of the friendship that shook South Africa and awakened the world

Twenty thousand mourners gather together to hear the speech at the funeral of black activist Steve Biko. They mourn his death and celebrate his life by singing the anthem "Nkosi Sikelel Afrika."

CRY FREEDOM, 1987

823 History's most seductive woman!

Cleopatra's seduction of Marc Antony on her splendid barge and her suicide from the bite of a snake were two of the most memorable scenes of director Cecil B. DeMille's career. However, one of the best and most telling moments comes from Julius Caesar's response here:

Cleopatra: "Together, we could conquer the world."

Caesar: "Nice of you to include me."

CLEOPATRA, 1934

824 The screen explodes with rage and passion and greatness!

The Archbishop of Canterbury (Richard Burton) and King Henry II (Peter O'Toole) are close friends and comrades. In one revealing scene, they take refuge from a rainstorm in a Saxon peasant's hut. The king, who believes that all Saxons are "dogs," lecherously eyes the peasant's daughter. When the Archbishop sees what is happening, he contrives to save the girl from the king's lust.

BECKET, 1964

825 The gladiator who defied an emperor

As rose petals fall on them from above, the gladiator hero Maximus and the corrupt, incestuous emperor Commodus are raised into the huge, bright arena surrounded by armed soldiers. The soldiers form a circle around them and the battle begins. Maximus, already wounded, drifts in and out of consciousness, but he fights bravely and manages to disarm the emperor. As the crowd shouts Maximus's name, Commodus calls for a sword, but his soldiers disobey him, leaving him unarmed. He pulls out a concealed blade, but Maximus fights back, twisting the weapon against his enemy, and killing him.

GLADIATOR, 2000

826 Income v. expenditure

Young David Copperfield's life brightens when he meets the ever-in-debt Mr. Micawber, who has this simple philosophy: "Annual income, twenty pounds; annual expenditure, nineteen and six; result, happiness. Annual income, twenty pounds; annual expenditure, twenty pounds and six; result, misery." David is sheltered by Micawber's large and loving family until the likeable man is carted off to debtor's prison.

DAVID COPPERFIELD, 1935

827 A story of The Christ. The glory of His spoken words.

This tale of the life of Christ is narrated by Orson Welles and is one of the most interesting biblical epics ever made. In the days after his crucifixion and resurrection, all of the sightings of Jesus are presented as second-hand information.

KING OF KINGS, 1961

828 Guilty until proven innocent

Young Englishwoman Adela Quested hopes to experience the real India while in Chandrapore, and she accepts Muslim Doctor Aziz's offer to visit the ancient Marabar caves. However, she has a strange and frightening experience inside the caves, and when she emerges, flustered and injured, she accuses the confused doctor of raping her.

A PASSAGE TO INDIA, 1984

829 "A mighty warrior"

Eccentric British officer T. E. Lawrence presses a plunger on the ridge of a sand dune, setting off an explosion that derails a Turkish train, then his Arab followers open fire. Lawrence shouts, "Stop it!" and runs into the line of fire, shooting off flares to get their attention. Then he gestures with his arm and leads a bloody assault down the dune.

LAWRENCE OF ARABIA, 1962

830 Homecoming

Gérard Depardieu is superb as the sixteenth-century war veteran. He struts confidently into the village he left years before, and is greeted by friends, family, and even his wife and child, who all accept him as their loved one returned home. But is this man really Martin Guerre?

THE RETURN OF MARTIN GUERRE, 1982

831 Cold-blooded killer

At the Plaszow Forced Labor Camp, Amon Goeth (Ralph Fiennes) watches the Jewish prisoners passing to and fro in front of his balcony. He takes out a high-velocity hunting rifle, raises it, and scans the people through its telescopic sight. The crosshairs settle on a woman who seems to be moving slightly more slowly than the others and he calmly squeezes off a single shot that kills her.

SCHINDLER'S LIST, 1993

832 A painful family secret

Queen Alexandra of Russia gains favor when she gives birth to the much-loved Prince Alexis, but this changes when it is discovered that Alexis suffers from hemophilia, a disease that runs in her family. Alexandra must then make the difficult decision to put her son's fate into the hands of mystical holy man Rasputin.

NICHOLAS AND ALEXANDRA, 1971

833 The most amazing conspiracy the world has ever known

Ingrid Bergman is rescued from committing suicide by Yul Brynner, who then schemes to have her accepted as the lost Princess Anastasia, the heir to the Russian throne, so he can collect the ten million pounds held in trust for her. As she learns how to be a convincing princess, it suddenly becomes clear that she instinctively knows more about Anastasia than she has been told.

ANASTASIA, 1956

834 Men are not animals

Demetrius, a Christian and former slave, is condemned to train as a gladiator. When he refuses to fight and tries to escape from the training school, he catches the attention of the beautiful Messalina:
Messalina: "We admire a magnificent animal who fights. Why not men?"
Demetrius: "Because God did not put men on earth to destroy his own kind. Nor a woman to enjoy their agonies as they die."

DEMETRIUS AND THE GLADIATORS, 1954

835 Morale booster

Henry V (Laurence Olivier), the recently crowned king of England, spends the evening before the battle with France incognito, mingling among his men and learning from them. This prompts him to give a speech that inspires his proud troops to march into battle prepared to die for their country.

HENRY V, 1944

836 The man...The music... The madness...The murder...

Wolfgang Amadeus Mozart is visited by a stranger wearing the same costume that Mozart's father wore before his death. The man commissions a requiem mass from the wayward musical genius and leaves him with some money—and very little time.

AMADEUS, 1984

837 "Don't follow the lights!"

Without a doubt, the *Lord of the Rings* trilogy will go down in history as *the* epic of this millennium. In one scene, Frodo Baggins is being guided through the endless Dead Marshes by the creature Gollum. Floating under the gloomy marsh waters are countless dead bodies and eerie lights, and Frodo, mesmerized, feels an overwhelming temptation to join them under the water and to give up the ring.

THE LORD OF THE RINGS: THE TWO TOWERS, 2002

838 Light your fires

Jean Seberg became a star thanks to this portrayal of the legendary French teenager, whose claim of hearing angels led to her taking command of an army. In one scene, she is offered the chance to avoid being burnt at the stake by renouncing her claims—she refuses.

SAINT JOAN, 1957

839 Mountainous seas and cracking timbers

In this nautical tale, Russell Crowe stars as Captain "Lucky" Jack Aubrey of the HMS *Surprise*. In one scene, his ship is attacked by the powerful French frigate the *Acheron*, which sneaks up on the crew in the fog and rains cannonballs down upon them, destroying their ship's masts and filling the air with the sound of splintering wood.

MASTER AND COMMANDER: THE FAR SIDE OF THE WORLD, 2003

840 Pomp and ruthlessness

Anne discovers letters written by her grandfather's first wife, Olivia, whose life has always been shrouded in secrecy and scandal. They reveal that, in her youth, the free-spirited woman had fallen in love with an Indian nobleman and had left her husband. The letters then lead Anne on a life-changing journey to India.

HEAT AND DUST, 1982

841 Akira Kurosawa's masterpiece

The great battle that concludes this film is one of the best ever filmed. The protagonists are compelled by custom to watch the battle from afar, and they sit on little stools, dressed in rags and clutching fans that look like lollipops. Meanwhile, the camera shows us image upon image of battle: bodies falling to the ground, great waves of men advancing to their inevitable deaths, and then the stillness, broken only by the occasional movements of a dying soldier or a wounded horse trying to get up onto its hooves.

KAGEMUSHA, 1980

842 A temptation no one could resist

Kate Croy has been forced to end her relationship with penniless journalist Merton Densher. When wealthy but terminally ill Millie Theale comes into their lives and displays her affection for Merton, Kate proposes a plan that will solve all her problems:

Merton: "You want me to seduce a dying girl? And what makes you think she'll just leave me all her money?"

Kate: "I know her. I know how she loves."

THE WINGS OF THE DOVE, 1997

843 The greatest story of love, faith, and overwhelming spectacle!

This somber epic dedicates an entire scene to Pontius Pilate (Richard Boone) washing his hands as he entreats Roman tribune Marcellus Gallio (Richard Burton) to supervise the crucifixion of Christ.

THE ROBE, 1953

844 The movie of your wildest dreams

Based on a fragment of a first-century text by Petronius, this surreal story is set in a world of magic, superstition, and hallucination. Every moment is a cinematic feast, including the comic legend of the Widow of Ephesus, which is pictured as it is told by a storyteller at a strange banquet.

SATYRICON, 1969

845 In sickness and in health

This historical saga recounts the events that led up to the crowning of Russia's Catherine the Great. In one scene, Empress Elizabeth (Catherine's mother-in-law) reveals her fears about her son's state of mind from her deathbed. Once she has died, Catherine is left to contend with her husband's cruel and irrational behavior alone.

CATHERINE THE GREAT, 1934

846 "God loves me. I know he loves me. I want him to stop."

The scene that caused protests in the streets was that of Christ's dream while on the cross. He imagines himself making love to Mary Magdalene, and having the companionship of a wife and family.

THE LAST TEMPTATION OF CHRIST, 1988

847 Devoted servant

Stevens (Anthony Hopkins) is the perfect British butler, but he is also completely closed off from any emotions that might distract him from his duties. In one scene, his dedication to service even keeps him from being with his dying father during his final moments.

THE REMAINS OF THE DAY, 1993

848 "He was not captured by force of arms, but by their softness."

Philistine Delilah holds Jewish champion Samson responsible for her sister's death, and she is determined to defeat him. The beguiling young woman uses all of her feminine wiles to woo the hero, until he finally reveals to her the secret of his great strength—his long hair.

SAMSON AND DELILAH, 1949

849 Words don't win wars.

Arrogant tyrant Hidetora has already married off his two eldest sons to the daughters of defeated chiefs, and he is now considering offers from two other warlords for their daughters to marry his youngest son, Saburo. The old man announces that he is retiring and that he will divide his lands among all three sons. He asks them to swear allegiance to him and to each other, but young Saburo refuses and is immediately banished.

RAN, 1985

850 All your expectations fulfilled

It is difficult to choose just one great moment of this wonderful film. Should it be the scene in which Pip is grabbed by an escaped convict on the lonely marshes and greets him with a mixture of fear and compassion? Or perhaps when he meets old Miss Havisham, who is covered with dust and cobwebs. She sits in her tattered wedding dress at the dining table which is still laid out for the wedding banquet that should have happened so long ago?

GREAT EXPECTATIONS, 1946

Family
Flicks

Family films are everyone's favorites. They allow adults and children to enjoy sharing the cinema experience together, whether in a movie theater or at home. These enchanting movies often show good triumphing over evil, and many teach wholesome family values, but the best of them manage to captivate young and old alike without being overly-sentimental or moralistic. Many family films are comic treats that make our sides split with laughter, while others are poignant movies with a high feel-good factor. But whatever their plots or themes, there will always be a place in our hearts for a wonderful family movie.

Previous page: Audrey Hepburn and Gregory Peck in *Roman Holiday* (1953).

851 The toys are back in town

Cowboy Woody, trying to convince him that he is a toy, presses
a button and opens the visor on Buzz Lightyear's space helmet.
Buzz writhes around in agony as if he is suffocating—
then suddenly realizes that he can breathe!

TOY STORY, 1995

852 Heart-melting

How could anyone's heart not lift when the young
pajama-clad boy and his friend, the snowman, take off
into the air on their magical adventure, accompanied
by the beautiful song "Walking in the Air"?

THE SNOWMAN, 1982

853 The movie with a 20,000-mile or one-million-laughs guarantee!

"The Great Leslie" and Professor Fate are stranded on a melting
iceberg. Out of earshot of the others, they discuss their predicament:
Leslie: "You better keep it to yourself."
Fate: "Oh, of course I'll keep it to myself. Until the water reaches my
lower lip, and then I'm going to mention it to somebody!"

THE GREAT RACE, 1965

854 A madcap frolic of crime and fun

Inspector Clouseau and his men stake out a costume party. Clouseau catches a sergeant, who is dressed as a zebra, drinking the punch, and says, "Any more behavior like this and I'll have your stripes!"

THE PINK PANTHER, 1964

855 A family comedy without the family

On the eve of a family vacation, eight-year-old Kevin (Macaulay Culkin) is sent to sleep in the loft for fighting. The next morning, as the family rush to catch their flight, they accidentally count the head of a neighbor passing by and don't realize that they are one person short. Kevin is left home alone—a fact he celebrates by bouncing on his parents' bed and eating a massive box of popcorn!

HOME ALONE, 1990

856 "What do girls do who haven't any mothers to help them through their troubles?"

This wonderful adaptation of Louisa May Alcott's tale of the four March sisters includes Katharine Hepburn's unforgettable performance as feisty, sharp-tongued Jo. The most moving scene of all is when Jo returns home to care for her weak and kindhearted sister, Beth (Jean Parker).

LITTLE WOMEN, 1933

857 They turned a lost island into an exotic paradise!

After a family is shipwrecked on a deserted tropical island, they realize that they must build themselves a shelter to live in—a tree house. The father (John Mills) does everything he can to keep his family's morale up: "The world is full of nice, ordinary little people who live in nice, ordinary little houses on the ground. Didn't you ever dream of a house in the trees?"

SWISS FAMILY ROBINSON, 1960

858 What if Peter Pan grew up?

Peter Pan (Robin Williams) has done what he promised he was never going to do—he has grown up! He is now a lawyer, and he has children of his own. When his children are kidnapped, his fairy friend Tinkerbell (Julia Roberts) arrives to take him back to Never Never Land, but first she has to get him to believe in her:

Peter: "You're a…you're a complex Freudian hallucination having something to do with my mother and I don't know why you have wings, but you have very lovely legs and you're a very nice, tiny person and, what am I saying, I don't know who my mother was; I'm an orphan and I've never done drugs because I missed the sixties…"

Tinkerbell: "Guess again."

HOOK, 1991

859 Go wild in the country!

In this definitive version of Kenneth Grahame's wonderful tale, it is great fun when Toad takes up driving. He is terrible at it, driving too fast and always crashing, but he takes great delight in being behind the wheel, and he joyfully calls out, "It's the only thing—Poop! Poop!"

THE WIND IN THE WILLOWS, 1996

860 "Grandfather...Grandfather..."

Heidi's cruel aunt comes to Grandfather's house in the mountains to take the little girl away to the big city. As she is driven away on the sled, Heidi turns, holds out her little arms, and, with her eyes full of tears, calls: "Grandfather...Grandfather...."

HEIDI, 1937

861 An unforgettable story of forty gallant years

In a Berlin restaurant, young Blimp, seeing a German who had been imprisoned in South Africa, asks the band to play a tune that used to be played in a South African prison. The enraged German pays the band to stop, but Blimp buys them all drinks to play the tune again. The cycle continues until each man is straining at the leash.

THE LIFE AND DEATH OF COLONEL BLIMP, 1943

862 Big Pajamas!

In this wonderful Marx Brothers film, Groucho's most celebrated character, Captain Spaulding, gives a compelling monologue about his exploits in Africa: "One morning I shot an elephant in my pajamas. How he got in my pajamas, I don't know."

ANIMAL CRACKERS, 1930

863 Heart and soul

One scene that is sheer delight is that of Tom Hanks, who plays Josh, a 12-year-old boy in the body of a 35-year-old man, performing "Chopsticks" with his boss MacMillan (Robert Loggia) by dancing on a giant piano keyboard on the floor of a toy store.

BIG, 1988

864 "Just like a doll's house"

The woodland animals lead Snow White to a small cottage. When she knocks at the tiny front door, there is no answer, so she lets herself in. Everything in the house is tiny, but it is also very dirty and untidy. When she counts seven small chairs, Snow White assumes that seven children live in the house, and she wonders why it is such a mess: "Why, you'd think their mother would—" Then it strikes her: "Maybe they have no mother."

SNOW WHITE AND THE SEVEN DWARFS, 1937

865 All sink together...

This wonderfully eccentric film is a real treat. Alastair Sim plays the seedy headmaster of a boarding school for boys, and Margaret Rutherford plays the no-nonsense headmistress of a girls' school, and the two are thrown together by a wartime mix-up. In one scene, the female teachers arrive, unaware that they have been moved to a boys' school. They enter the dining hall and are faced with a coat of arms bearing the motto "Guard Thine Honour."

THE HAPPIEST DAYS OF YOUR LIFE, 1950

866 A movie about those who appreciate the finest things in life...for free!

An art forger's daughter, Nicole Bonnet (Audrey Hepburn), wishes to emphasize her point, so she firmly grasps her father (Peter O'Toole) by his chin hair and leads him across the room:

Nicole Bonnet: "I keep telling you, when you sell a fake masterpiece, it's a crime!"

Charles Bonnet: "But I don't sell them to poor people—only to millionaires."

HOW TO STEAL A MILLION, 1966

867 Not something you see every day

On a beautiful, bright morning, two microlight aircraft take off and lead a flock of orphaned geese through the sky. For a moment they become lost in the poor visibility of the clouds. Then they emerge to find themselves flying along the main street of downtown Baltimore. People watch in disbelief from the windows of the high-rise office buildings as the gaggle of geese and gliders pass by.

FLY AWAY HOME, 1996

868 Divine intervention

In a cross-channel air race, the Italian pilot's plane comes down in a field because of a fuel blockage. He repairs it, but he can't take off without help. When a group of nuns arrive to tell him to go away, he asks for their help, and they almost refuse:

Count Emilio Ponticelli: "It is a pity that the race will now be won by a Protestant."

Mother Superior: "A Protestant? Sisters, don't stand there gazing. This good Catholic needs our help!"

THOSE MAGNIFICENT MEN IN THEIR FLYING MACHINES, 1965

869 That's amore

Two dogs sit at a table outside an Italian restaurant, where the kind chef serves them a huge plate of spaghetti and meatballs. As the dogs slurp up the same piece of spaghetti while gazing into each other's eyes, their lips suddenly meet in an unexpected kiss.

LADY AND THE TRAMP, 1955

870 Hip hip hooray!

In the summer of 1929, a mother lets her four children sail over to the nearby island in their little boat, *Swallow* to set up camp. The children soon realize they have landed in rival *Amazon* territory and the scene is set for a summer of rivalry, fun, and adventure.

SWALLOWS AND AMAZONS, 1974

871 "Fair dinkum"

A group of drunken local boys are taking potshots at kangaroos at night from their truck in the Australian outback. Mick Dundee grabs one of the dead animals and hides behind it, placing his own rifle in its arm. When the vehicle's headlights fall on the armed kangaroo, the animal appears to be preparing to shoot back at them, and the horrified youths flee with their tails between their legs!

CROCODILE DUNDEE, 1986

872 A topsy-turvy world

This magical adventure is full of great moments, but one of the most unforgettable is when the White Rabbit simply says to Alice, "Don't just do something; stand there!"

ALICE IN WONDERLAND, 1951

873 You've got to hand it to him

Audrey Hepburn plays a princess who escapes from her bodyguards to explore Rome. Reporter Gregory Peck shows her the sights, but keeps his identity secret in hope of getting a scoop. In one great scene, the couple visits a sculpture called *The Mouth of Truth*. Peck tests the sculpture's ancient legend by putting his hand into the mouth. He pretends that his hand is bitten off, which shocks Hepburn, then sends her into a fit of laughter.

ROMAN HOLIDAY, 1953

874 Shell-shocked...

Daryl Hannah plays a mermaid who comes to New York to search for a man (Tom Hanks) that she rescued from drowning. In one scene, he takes her to an elegant restaurant, where she grabs the lobster off her plate, rips into it, and eats it—shell and all—with her hands.

SPLASH, 1984

875 "I'm going to be king of Pride Rock."

Simba's father, King Mufasa, shows him around the kingdom he will one day inherit. Simba then pays a visit to his greedy, evil uncle Scar, who became second in line to the throne when young Simba was born.
Simba: "Hey, Uncle Scar, when I'm king, what'll that make you?"
Scar: "A monkey's uncle."
Simba: "You're so weird."
Scar: "You have no idea."

THE LION KING, 1994

876 First comes love. Then comes the interrogation.

When Greg Focker meets his girlfriend's parents for the first time, things don't go according to plan. Her highly suspicious father, former CIA agent Jack Byrnes, is an experienced interrogator:
Jack Byrnes: "I'm just curious—did you pick the color of the car?"
Greg Focker: "Uh, no, the guy at the window did. Why?"
Jack Byrnes: "Well, they say geniuses pick green."
Greg Focker: "Oh."
Jack Byrnes: "But you didn't pick it."

MEET THE PARENTS, 2000

877 He doesn't just talk to the animals!

One night, Dr. John Dolittle (Eddie Murphy) nearly runs over a dog with his car. The dog yells, "Bonehead!" at him, then disappears—and from that point on, Dolittle can understand everything animals say. Later, when he meets the dog again, he asks its name. The dog describes the time he came closest to being given a name: "A little girl once called me 'Please, Mommy, not him.'"

DOCTOR DOLITTLE, 1998

878 "Who's Harvey?"

Elwood P. Dowd is a pleasant and mild-mannered man who just happens, so he says, to have as his invisible friend a six-foot-tall rabbit named Harvey! In one scene, he talks to Harvey at a bar, and the two leave together like a pair of old pals.

HARVEY, 1950

879 This ain't no chick flick!

Rocky, the flying rooster, is relaxing in a whirlpool bath while running a training session for the chickens. He tells the chicken massaging his back, "Down a bit...now little circles...faster..." unaware that the other chickens are running themselves into the ground, thinking that he is still conducting training exercises.

CHICKEN RUN, 2000

880 Double trouble

Two little girls, both beautifully played by Hayley Mills, meet at summer camp, and are shocked to see that they look alike. They soon realize that they are twins, and they come up with a plan to reunite their parents:

Sharon: "If we switched, sooner or later, they'd have to unswitch us."

Susan: "Mother would have to bring me to California to unmix us."

Sharon: "And they'd have to meet again."

Susan: "Face-to-face. Are you thinking what I'm thinking?"

THE PARENT TRAP, 1961

881 "What's in a name? That which we call a rose by an other name would smell as sweet."

In this beautifully animated classic, mischievous rabbit Thumper teaches newborn deer Bambi how to walk and talk, and he shows him around the forest. When they come upon a skunk, a simple mix-up gives the shy animal a new name:

Bambi: "Butterfly!"

Thumper: "Nope…that's a flower."

Bambi: [runs into a skunk] "Flower?"

Thumper: [laughing] "That's not a flower!"

Flower: "That's all right. He can call me Flower if he wants to."

BAMBI, 1942

882 Somewhere inside all of us is the power to change the world

Matilda Wormwood is a very gifted little girl, but her parents don't know it—they are too busy ignoring her and watching television. One day she asks her father for a book:

Harry: "A book? What do you want a book for?"

Matilda: "To read."

Harry: "To read? Why would you want to read when you got the television set sitting right in front of you? There's nothing you can get from a book that you can't get from a television faster."

MATILDA, 1996

883 All for one and one for all!

The three musketeers have rescued their new young friend D'Artagnan from execution and are fleeing from the cardinal's guards in the cardinal's own horse-drawn coach. Rummaging around in the back, Porthos discovers a picnic basket, and he offers a drink to Athos, who is driving:

Porthos: "Champagne?"

Athos: "We're in the middle of a chase, Porthos."

Porthos: "You're right—something red."

THE THREE MUSKETEERS, 1993

884 Splat!

This film, which has an entire cast of children playing gangsters and nightclub workers, has a shootout in the club as its fantastically fun climax, in which everyone gets creamed by splurge guns.

BUGSY MALONE, 1976

885 "But I think I will have seen everything, when I see an elephant fly."

The little elephant is pushed from the burning house in the circus tent. He desperately tries to grab onto the magic feather with his trunk—and suddenly, he begins to fly, soaring high above the heads of the surprised clowns and audience!

DUMBO, 1941

886 Bon appétit

Two boys who have been turned into mice by a witch use the woman's own potion against her. They lace the soup with the magical ingredient just before it is served to her and the other witches, who are all in disguise. The witches are turned into rodents, and are systematically dispatched by the hotel staff.

THE WITCHES, 1990

887 Birthday dreams

Jenny Agutter plays Bobbie Waterbury, one of three children forced to move to a country cottage when their father is arrested. In one scene, Bobbie enters the room on her birthday to discover that it is filled with loving friends bearing gifts, and she glides through the room to each of them in an overwhelmed, dreamlike state.

THE RAILWAY CHILDREN, 1970

888 "La bella luna!"

Grandfather takes the dogs for a walk to show them "la bella luna," the beautiful moon. They begin to howl up at the moon like little wolves, and the old man laughs like a youngster again.

MOONSTRUCK, 1987

889 The greatest rock-and-roll comedy adventure

Wilfrid Brambell steals the show from the Beatles as Paul's grandfather. He is always searching for an opportunity to misbehave and, in one scene, he pockets a casino invitation that arrives for the boys. When they leave, the grandfather borrows a suit from a waiter, who arrives with room service, and goes out on the town.

A HARD DAY'S NIGHT, 1964

890 Smashing

Charlie Chaplin comes up with a money-making ploy—he will get a kid to break someone's window, and then he will conveniently turn up shortly afterward, armed with a pane of glass and some putty.

THE KID, 1921

891 The little darlings

A group of crooks returns to the mansion where they stashed the loot from a train robbery, only to discover that the building has been taken over by St. Trinian's Girls' School. They are given a wonderful send-off by the little she-devils, who are armed with hockey sticks.

THE GREAT ST. TRINIAN'S TRAIN ROBBERY, 1966

892 "Life is like a box of chocolates, you never know what you're gonna get."

As a child, Forrest Gump is fitted with leg braces to straighten him out. One day he is threatened by bullies, and his friend, Jenny, urges him to run. As he does so, his leg braces begin to fall into pieces on the road, leaving him free to run like the wind.

FORREST GUMP, 1994

893 Quit while you're ahead

This delightful movie is ideal for a rainy day. In one scene, sales executive David Niven gives nonsmoker Shirley MacLaine a new brand of cigarette to try. She takes it, tries to make an impression, takes one puff, and launches into a hilarious coughing fit. She eventually recovers and then tries another brand—with the same result.

ASK ANY GIRL, 1959

894 One ring to rule them all

The wizard Gandalf stands in Bilbo Baggins's small home and tries to convince him to leave his strange ring behind when he goes on his journey, but the Hobbit is under the ring's spell, and he will not be easily parted from it.

Bilbo: "It's mine...my own...my Precious."

Gandalf: "Precious? It's been called that before, but not by you."

Bilbo: "Oh, what business is it of yours what I do with my things?"

Gandalf: "I think you've had that ring quite long enough."

Bilbo: "You...you want it for yourself!"

Gandalf: "BILBO BAGGINS! Do not take me for some conjurer of cheap tricks! I am not trying to rob you, I'm trying to help you!"

THE LORD OF THE RINGS: THE FELLOWSHIP OF THE RING, 2001

895 The oddest couple ever unleashed!

Detective Scott Turner (Tom Hanks) is on a stakeout with big, lumbering, slobbering, wrinkle-faced dog Hooch. Turner starts talking to the dog and goofing around. When Hooch shakes his head furiously, Turner tries it, too—and becomes incredibly dizzy.

TURNER AND HOOCH, 1989

896 We think they are scary, but really we scare them!

The monsters of the city of Monstropolis get the fright of their lives when they discover that a small child has entered their world through her closet door. They believe that there is "nothing more toxic or deadly than a human child."

MONSTERS, INC. 2001

897 I'll take mine black

Agent K (Tommy Lee Jones) shows skeptical new recruit James Edwards (Will Smith) around his workplace. James refuses to believe anything he has been told about aliens living on Earth, so K takes him to the coffee room. They walk into a room full of strange, insectlike aliens who are drinking coffee, smoking cigarettes, and shooting the breeze.

MEN IN BLACK, 1997

898 Just peachy

The moment when James goes inside the giant peach and escapes his
dreadful aunts is wonderful. He is transformed into an animation, and
he meets the unusual characters who will share in his epic journey.

JAMES AND THE GIANT PEACH, 1996

899 "Some day you'll learn that greatness is only the seizing of opportunity…"

The greatest moment in this inspirational movie is Mickey Rooney's
heartfelt confession that he has had a terrible fear of horses ever
since he was in a race in which another jockey was killed.

NATIONAL VELVET, 1944

900 Saved by the relics of our history

The German army has invaded England and locked novice witch
Angela Lansbury and three young evacuees in an old castle, which
is crammed with ancient suits of armor, weapons, banners, and
marching drums. Lansbury recites a magic spell, and the flags
begin to flutter and the drums begin to sound. Soon she has a vast,
ghostly army under her control, and she leads them into battle.

BEDKNOBS AND BROOMSTICKS, 1971

Tearjerkers

What is it about certain movies that moves viewers all around the world? In the main, it seems to be loss—the loss of love or loved-ones, or perhaps the loss of hope, freedom, or a way of life. But it can also be the happy moments—when loved-ones are reunited, or when we are surprised that everything has turned out well. However, it isn't only traditional melodramas that tug at our heartstrings; we are sometimes induced to tears by the most unexpected films. This chapter describes poignant scenes from a variety of movie genres, recognizing that while some of us may weep at *Terms of Endearment* or *Titanic*, others will shed a tear or two while watching *Top Gun* or *The Great Escape*.

Previous page: Maureen O'Hara and Roddy McDowall in
How Green Was My Valley (1941).

901 Follow your heart

Poor George Emerson desperately tries to win Lucy Honeychurch's heart and to tear her away from her stoic fiancé, Cecil Vyse: "He doesn't know what a woman is. He wants you as a possession, something to own. He doesn't love you."

A ROOM WITH A VIEW, 1985

902 There is no such thing as a simple miracle

The scene in which Leonard Lowe's mother (Ruth Nelson) sees her son (Robert De Niro) awake, after being in a comatose state for decades, always brings out the handkerchiefs in the cinema.

AWAKENINGS, 1990

903 Nothing on Earth could come between them

In a fantasy scene, 101-year-old Rose returns to being her beautiful 17-year-old self. She climbs up the opulent Grand Staircase on the Titanic to be reunited with her lover, Jack, who is waiting for her at the clock with all of the other passengers who perished with him on that fateful night.

TITANIC, 1997

904 Almost surreal

In a horrific battle scene that takes the viewer right into the action, hundreds of soldiers storm Omaha Beach as part of the D-Day landings. Amid the chaos and carnage, a dazed young soldier can be seen walking along the beach—he is looking for his arm.

SAVING PRIVATE RYAN, 1998

905 And then they were gone

In a surprisingly poignant moment at the end of this movie, the little girl, Boo, opens her closet door and finds it empty.

MONSTERS, INC. 2001

906 He was their inspiration. He made their lives extraordinary.

In the final scene, the boys are instructed to ignore their departing teacher (Robin Williams) as he leaves the classroom, but, one by one, they stand on their desks in defiance, face their mentor, and pledge their loyalty: "Captain, my captain!" He looks at them admiringly and simply says, "Thank you, boys. Thank you."

DEAD POETS SOCIETY, 1989

907 "This mission is over!"

After being compelled to give himself up by his former colonel, Samuel Trautman, war veteran and hero John Rambo delivers a magnificent speech:

Trautman: "It's over, Johnny. It's over!"

Rambo: "Nothing is over! Nothing! You just don't turn it off!"

FIRST BLOOD, 1982

908 They broke his heart. But they couldn't break his spirit.

If you take the time to watch this little gem of a movie, I guarantee that you will tremble when Casper discovers wild Kestrel Kes in the garbage can.

KES, 1969

909 "Man was in the forest."

Spring returns to the forest. Bambi's mother takes her son out onto the meadow, but man also enters the forest, and the two deer run into the thicket. Gunshots are heard. Bambi escapes and calls to his mother, whom he assumes is right behind him, "We made it!" he exclaims. "We made it, Mother! We? Mother?" His mother is no longer with him.

BAMBI, 1942

910 Two men chasing dreams of glory!

Sam sets about showing Harold why he lost his race. He explains, "Remember, overstriding. Death for the sprinter…knocks you back." He slaps Harold across the cheek. "Like that!" he says, as he slaps him again. "And that!" Then he laughs and takes Harold by the arm.

CHARIOTS OF FIRE, 1981

911 A Los Angeles crime saga

After a lengthy car chase, detective Al Pacino pursues thief Robert De Niro on foot onto an airport runway. De Niro dies on a grassy runway shoulder, having been shot by Pacino, who holds his adversary's hand as he dies.

HEAT, 1995

912 On the border of Switzerland

After the small plane in which they escaped crashes on a hillside, American pilot James Garner sends blind forger Donald Pleasence away from the plane. The two men almost made it to freedom—but, as Pleasence walks away, a platoon of Nazis, of which he is completely unaware, opens fire and kills him.

THE GREAT ESCAPE, 1963

913 Her greatest talent was for life

Sobering, enchanting, and finely acted, this wonderful movie portrays the selfless devotion of John Bayley to his difficult wife, Iris Murdoch, as she travels along the degenerative path of Alzheimer's Disease.

Iris: "I...wrote?"
John: "Yes, my darling, clever cat! You wrote books."
Iris: "Books? I wrote?"

IRIS, 2001

914 In memory, love lives forever.

Hungarian explorer Count Laszlo de Almásy must leave his lover, Katharine Clifton, alone in a cave with her broken legs, a flashlight, a pencil, and very little else while he walks into the endless desert to find help. Their parting is immeasurably poignant:

Katharine: "Promise me you'll come back for me."
Laszlo: "I promise, I'll come back for you. I promise, I'll never leave you."

THE ENGLISH PATIENT, 1996

915 His whole life was a million-to-one shot

Everyone is entitled to love or hate any film, but who could not be moved when boxing bum Rocky Balboa rises to the challenge, training his heart out, then running up the steps of city hall to raise his hands in triumph?

ROCKY, 1976

916 Take a handkerchief

This Richard Attenborough masterpiece is full of moving moments. The scene in which the boy, desperate to save his mother, rifles through the hanging furs in the attic in an effort to find the passage into the magical world of Narnia is absolutely heartbreaking.

SHADOWLANDS, 1993

917 A dying wish

Joe cannot bear to be away from pretty manicurist Sally and, even though he is in prison, his love remains strong. He manages to escape, and he heads for her cottage, unable to live without her, but the police catch up with him. They open fire, and he is mortally wounded, but at least poor Joe gets his one wish fulfilled—he dies in Sally's arms.

A COTTAGE ON DARTMOOR, 1929

918 A long time ago in a galaxy far, far away...

After battles galore in their struggle to uphold good in the fight against the Dark Side, Han Solo, Luke Skywalker, and Chewbacca proudly walk between the assembled troops of the rebel alliance, and are presented with medals by Princess Leia, as the familiar theme music swells.

STAR WARS, 1977

919 What if...

Jesus realizes on the cross that he has not betrayed his destiny, and he rejoices. Then we watch as he gently slips away, to the sound of the women's traditional mourning cries, as the film burns to white.

THE LAST TEMPTATION OF CHRIST, 1988

920 For those in peril on the sea

This enthralling true-life drama based on the sinking of the *Titanic* is an amazingly gripping and accurate portrayal of human tragedy. In the film, the small musical ensemble continues to play right up to the very end, just as the musicians did on the real ship as it sank—I shiver even now to think of it.

A NIGHT TO REMEMBER, 1958

921 He may never walk again

Young Huw's mother slips down a steep, icy embankment into a pond. Huw goes to her rescue and holds her head above the freezing water until his brothers save them. The next day, however, the boy overhears the doctor talking about him: "His legs were frozen to the bone. A year, two years, quiet like that. But I can't promise that he'll ever walk again. Nature must take her course."

HOW GREEN WAS MY VALLEY, 1941

922 It takes a strong man to save himself, and a great man to save another.

Prison comrades Andy and Red are reunited in Mexico as free men.

THE SHAWSHANK REDEMPTION, 1994

923 "You gotta let him go."

Anyone who dedicates a couple of hours to watching this movie will find it difficult not to shed a tear or two when Maverick (Tom Cruise) holds his best friend, Goose (Anthony Edwards), in his arms as he dies, surrounded by his parachute in the middle of the sea.

TOP GUN, 1986

924 "There's no place like home."

Professor Marvel tells young runaway Dorothy Gale to close her eyes and concentrate as he sneaks a peek into her little basket to find a photograph of her Auntie Em. He describes Dorothy's heartbroken aunt looking out into the distance for her missing niece, and Dorothy resolves to return home at once.

THE WIZARD OF OZ, 1939

925 "Let justice be done."

In an incredibly touching moment, District Attorney Jim Garrison's voice begins to crack with emotion during his summation of his case for conspiracy in the killing of President John F. Kennedy.

JFK, 1991

926 "Stop all the clocks..."

If the four weddings of the title are good fun and frolics, then the funeral of Gareth (Simon Callow), good friend to many and lover to one, is absolutely heart-wrenching, and serves to remind us all of our own mortality. John Hannah, as Matthew, gives a sincere eulogy that is one of the most affecting ever seen on screen.

FOUR WEDDINGS AND A FUNERAL, 1993

927 Ever heard of the expression, "things just go from bad to worse?"

Frank has seen his baby sister die, his dad fall to drink, his younger siblings destroyed by poverty, his mother ravaged by a relative; and his lover die of consumption. When he discovers a hoard of cash hidden at a local moneylender's home after she dies, we weep with relief. He heads for America, and, we hope, for a new and better life!

ANGELA'S ASHES, 1999

928 Who will survive in one of the greatest escape adventures ever?

In a selfless act, lovable mother figure Shelley Winters sacrifices herself for the sake of the others who are trying to find an escape route from the bowels of the sinking ship.

THE POSEIDON ADVENTURE, 1972

929 It's about life. It's about love. It's about us.

Abused Celie's sole consolation and friend is her sister Nettie, but when Nettie rejects Albert's lewd advances, he separates them, ripping them from each other. Nettie runs along the road, shouting to her sister and promising that she will write: "Nothing but death can keep me from it!"

THE COLOR PURPLE, 1985

930 Sal's farewell

Jim (James Dean) fails to save young Plato (Sal Mineo)—the boy who once said to him, "If only you coulda been my dad. We could have breakfast in the morning"—from a cop's deadly bullet.

REBEL WITHOUT A CAUSE, 1955

931 Melting moment

In a beautifully atmospheric moment, snow falls on Takashi Shimura as he slowly swings back and forth in the children's playground, singing to himself, "Life is so short / Fall in love, dear maiden / While your lips are still red / And before you are cold, / For there will be no tomorrow."

IKIRU, 1952

932 All his life, Ray Kinsella was searching for his dreams. Then one day, his dreams came looking for him.

Ray Kinsella's voice cracks as he asks the ghost of his deceased baseball-obsessed father to do something with him that Ray had always refused to do: "Hey, Dad? You wanna have a catch?" John Kinsella simply and honestly replies, "I'd like that."

FIELD OF DREAMS, 1989

933 Desperate measures

Cambodian man Dith Pran is captured by the Khmer Rouge while assisting American journalist Sydney Schanberg. Desperate to survive, Pran sneaks silently past the guards to a tethered cow, and makes a small incision in its neck with a razor blade. He drinks just enough of its blood to keep both himself and the animal alive.

THE KILLING FIELDS, 1984

934 For anyone who has ever wished upon a star

Can anyone watch as wooden puppet Pinocchio magically becomes a real boy and not well up?

PINOCCHIO, 1940

935 A mother's anguish

Doting mother Shirley MacLaine frantically seeks medical help to relieve the pain her terminally ill daughter is suffering. She runs completely around the nurse's station, desperately saying, "It's past 10:00. She's in pain. My daughter is in pain. Give her the shot. Do you understand me? Give my daughter the shot!"

TERMS OF ENDEARMENT, 1983

936 Peachy drops in on Kipling

Peachy Carnehan comes into Rudyard Kipling's study, dirty and dressed like a native, to deliver a golden crown and the wrapped head of the man who wore it—his comrade, Daniel Dravot. As Kipling looks upon it, Peachy recalls Daniel's fall from the rope bridge into the deep valley below: "It took him half an hour to fall."

THE MAN WHO WOULD BE KING, 1975

937 He is afraid. He is alone. He is three million light years from home.

Elliott and his alien friend are inextricably linked—when E.T. becomes dangerously ill, Elliott also gets sick, in a truly distressing scene.

E.T. THE EXTRA-TERRESTRIAL, 1982

938 A few words from mom

This classic drama of self-sacrifice, loyalty, and courage is just seventeen minutes long, and it pays tribute to the Londoners who endured the Nazi blitz during World War II. Even the stiffest upper lip will quiver as Celia Johnson, as an English mother, writes to her children, who have been evacuated to the United States.

A LETTER FROM HOME, 1941

939 Whoever saves one life, saves the world entire.

This incredible movie contains countless poignant scenes, but the most heart-wrenching moment has to be the final scene. The actors are joined by the real people they portrayed in the film to place stones on the grave of Oskar Schindler, the man who saved their lives.

SCHINDLER'S LIST, 1993

940 There's no escaping it

Anthony Perkins sits on the bed with his wife and newborn baby, holding a small box of pills. He explains to his wife that they are for when the time comes—for the time when the radioactive cloud that has killed everyone in every other country eventually reaches them...

ON THE BEACH, 1959

941 No one was prepared for this storm

It is difficult to decide which is the most distressing moment in this true story, as the image of Captain Billy Tyne (George Clooney) going down with his sinking trawler is as touching as the memorial service that follows.

A PERFECT STORM, 2000

942 Life's greatest adventure is finding your place in the Circle of Life

Lion cub Simba watches in terror as his father, Mufasa, falls to his death. He is then made to believe that he is to blame for the tragedy.

THE LION KING, 1994

943 Inside every one of us is a special talent waiting to come out. The trick is finding it.

Break out the tissues for the end of *Billy Elliot*, when the young ballet dancer's coal-miner father comes to London to see his son dance on stage.

BILLY ELLIOT, 2000

944 Pass the warning

Donald Sutherland sprints the length of the garden and plunges into the murky pond waters to pull out, in painful, wrenching slow motion, the drowned body of his little girl, whom we had seen playing only moments before.

DON'T LOOK NOW, 1973

945 "And death shall have no dominion."

Nina is so in love with Jamie and so determined not to let him go that his ghost returns to live with her. Day by day, he brings more new friends with him. Nina finds herself caught between the absurdity of the situation and her immense grief: "I can't believe I have a bunch of dead people watching videos in my living room."

TRULY, MADLY, DEEPLY, 1991

946 Priceless

Ivy St. Helier, as Manon La Crevette, gives a heartrending performance of the classic song "If Love Were All" in Noel Coward's musical tearjerker.

BITTER SWEET, 1933

947 A picture says a thousand words

The ending of this great comic drama, in which, Warren Schmidt (Jack Nicholson) receives a picture from the African child he sponsors, will make anyone weep.

ABOUT SCHMIDT, 2002

948 A fitting tribute to one of their own

The fireman's funeral on the streets of Chicago, shown at the end of this spectacular movie, has to be one of the saddest funeral scenes ever filmed.

BACKDRAFT, 1991

949 At the edge of the world, his journey begins.

Wilson, Chuck Noland's only friend on a deserted island, floats helplessly away from the raft on which they are escaping, leaving Chuck utterly alone as he calls out in anguish, "Wilson! Wilson! I'm sorry!"

CAST AWAY, 2000

950 A father's love

The legal system seems determined not to adequately punish two white men who raped a little black girl and left her for dead. As they're being marched into the courtroom for their arraignment, the girl's distraught father, Carl Lee Hailey, takes the law into his own hands and guns them down.

A TIME TO KILL, 1996

Mystery

Mystery and suspense films are the crosswords, puzzles, and riddles of the cinema. They set us on edge, light the fuses in our imaginations, and spark our investigative instincts. We each identify with the detective or curious hero, and we attempt to solve the mystery from the comfort and safety of our armchairs. Suspense is the key to keeping us hooked, and it usually builds and builds to an explosive climax full of revelations. Some of these movies are complex, or have endings that turn out to be nothing like we imagined, while others—the ones we adore watching over and over again—are fairly clear-cut from the start. Why do we love them so much? It's a mystery...

Previous page: Jane Wyman and Richard Todd in *Stage Fright* (1950).

436

951 The body was AWOL...
and a house party was on the loose!

Newspaper magnate Henry Kruger discovers the dead body of his bitter rival, Andy McDonald, in the back of his car. He enlists his chauffeur, Mack Hogan, to help him lose the body to avoid being implicated in the murder—but it doesn't stay lost for long!

THE MISSING CORPSE, 1945

952 Culture vulture

In one telling scene of this complex and erotic mystery, wealthy industrialist Harrison Shelgrove expounds his theory that ripping the hearts out of his victims is justifiable, because it is for the good cause of extending the lives of senior Republicans and the social elite!

SUNSET GRILL, 1992

953 If you knew what he knew,
what would you do?

A priest (Montgomery Clift) hears the confession of his church sexton (O. E. Hasse) who whispers through the grille in a tight close-up, "I...killed...a man." Bound by the laws of the confessional, he cannot inform the police of what he has heard.

I CONFESS, 1953

954 The maddest love that ever possessed a woman

There is a wonderful dream sequence by surrealist artist Salvador Dali in this Ingrid Bergman classic, which also stars Gregory Peck as a handsome psychiatrist who becomes the new director of a top-class mental asylum.

SPELLBOUND, 1945

955 Erotically charged

Attractive orphan Ivy (Drew Barrymore) wins a scholarship to an exclusive private school, which wealthy Sylvie (Sara Gilbert) also attends. In one scene, Ivy overhears Sylvie telephoning a phony bomb threat into the television station where her father works, and she decides to become friends with the reclusive teenager.

POISON IVY, 1992

956 Chaos unearthed

A Jerusalem shopkeeper discovers a tomb containing the crucified remains of a man. Rumors suggesting that it may be the body of Jesus Christ begin to spread. Soon everyone from archaeologists to the Israeli authorities have an opinion on the matter, and the Vatican sends Father Gutierrez (Antonio Banderas) to investigate.

THE BODY, 2001

957 Everything covered except...

Idealistic young reporter Jim Baldwin sets out to unmask an unfair legal system by planting circumstantial evidence to implicate himself in the death of a colleague, who goes into hiding until the story goes public. But when his hidden friend really does get killed, poor Jim becomes the prime suspect!

CIRCUMSTANTIAL EVIDENCE, 1935

958 Is there anybody there?

In this low-budget murder mystery, quick-witted police detective Devlin must unravel the mystery of why a hated millionaire was murdered with a rare, oriental dagger during a séance. It soon becomes clear that everyone present had sufficient motive.

SINISTER HANDS, 1932

959 How much do you know about your uncle?

A young girl is overjoyed when her favorite uncle comes to visit, but she becomes suspicious of him when he cuts out and hides an article from the evening newspaper. She visits the library and locates the missing article. The headline reads:
WHO IS THE MERRY WIDOW MURDERER?

SHADOW OF A DOUBT, 1943

960 A jewel of a mystery-thriller

The scene is a Hong Kong park. A woman sits on a park bench…a man brushes against her…she slips to the ground…dead…murdered. Then the man is also killed.

RED DRAGON, 1965

961 West meets East

This underrated gem focuses on American Harry Kilmer's (Robert Mitchum) efforts to find his friend's daughter, who has been kidnapped. The moment in which he sits opposite his old nemesis, Tanaka, slices off his own finger, and presents it to him, wrapped in a white handkerchief, is filled with the mystery of the East.

THE YAKUZA, 1975

962 Clowning around

Andrew Wyke (Laurence Olivier) invites Milo Tindle (Michael Caine), who is having an affair with his wife, to his house. He proposes that Milo stage a burglary, so that Andrew can claim the insurance money and thereby cover his alimony expenses when he grants his wife a divorce. When Milo reluctantly agrees, Andrew takes him to rummage through a trunk full of costumes, and pulls out an embarrassing circus-clown disguise for Milo to wear.

SLEUTH 1972

963 Game, set, and match

In the establishing scene of this suspense-filled Hitchcock classic, celebrity tennis pro Guy Haines meets a mysterious playboy named Bruno Anthony onboard a train. They engage in small talk, discussing Haines's troubled marriage and Anthony's hatred for his father. Anthony jokes that they could "exchange murders," which turns out to be a plausible notion. There would be nothing to link the two men and their victims; who would ever know?

STRANGERS ON A TRAIN, 1951

964 You can't escape what you can't see

When his policeman father fails to discover who is attacking blind people, a small boy named Lucas, fearing that his mother may be the next victim, begins his own secret investigations. When he eventually comes face-to-face with the "slasher," Lucas stabs him through the eye with a knitting needle—but the movie then takes an unexpected turn.

AFRAID OF THE DARK, 1991

965 His guilt is as clear as a bell

In small-town America, a pipe-smoking stranger named Wilson moves in on a man named Dr. Rankin, who is suspected of war crimes. He shows Rankin's girlfriend, Mary, film footage shot at the concentration camps, but she refuses to believe that Rankin is guilty, and she rushes off to the clock tower to confront him. At 11:00 p.m., the clock chimes for the first time in years, and the entire town seems to come out to bear witness...

THE STRANGER, 1946

966 Living with a roommate can be murder

Allie Jones (Bridget Fonda) thinks that she has found the perfect roommate in shy Hedra Carlson (Jennifer Jason Leigh), until Hedra starts to take an unusual interest in her—first borrowing her clothes, then copying her mannerisms and hairstyle. When this interest becomes a frightening obsession, Allie asks Hedra to leave, and the situation takes a violent turn:
Allie: "I know you weren't yourself when you did this, Hedy."
Hedra: "I know. I was you."

SINGLE WHITE FEMALE, 1992

967 She was seduced into a world of sexual adventure...and dangerous deception.

Something very sinister has been going on at a psychiatric treatment center, and Kay Egan (Tanya Roberts) goes undercover as a nurse to find out how her sister died there. In one erotic scene, she discovers—through personal experience—that Jessica Callister (Delia Sheppard), who runs the center, is a highly-charged bisexual who preys on the pretty female nurses who work there.

SINS OF DESIRE, 1993

968 Innocents abroad

Two quintessential British cricket fans, Charters and Caldicott, are onboard a train carrying Nazis, impersonators pretending to be Nazis, spies, and counterspies, and they provide a welcome moment of light relief. Charters tells Caldicott that he has bought a copy of a book called *Mein Kampf*: "I understand they give a copy to all the bridal couples over here." Caldicott replies, "Oh, I don't think it's that sort of book, old man."

NIGHT TRAIN TO MUNICH, 1940

969 It's all about trying to remember

American agent Clayton Pierce, who has infiltrated a cell of Russian and Saudi gangsters, discovers that the briefcase he thought was filled with heroin is actually a thermonuclear device capable of destroying an entire city. Just what was in the drug administered to him by his own agency—and why is his memory fading?

TIME LAPSE, 2001

970 Red herrings galore

A Scotland Yard inspector is called in to investigate a series of killings. Initially he comes up with more questions than answers. Just what are those stains on the victims' carpets? What, exactly, is the murder weapon? And what possible link is there between the crimes and the mysterious people who have recently arrived from India?

THE CARPET OF HORROR, 1962

971 Little lies

Young Philippe, who idolizes his butler Baines, tries to deceive the police in order to protect Baines when he suspects him of being involved in his own wife's death. The crucial scene is that of the youth facing the impossible task of trying to get an adult to listen to his vital testimony.

THE FALLEN IDOL, 1948

972 But who had a hand in it?

In one horrifying scene set during World War II, a group of Japanese soldiers capture a British captain and his two men. The two soldiers refuse to give their interrogators the information they want, so they chop off their right hands. However, when the captain is tortured, he tells them everything they want to know, in order to save his own hand.

THE HAND, 1960

973 A card cheat was hung…then all hell broke loose!

Gambler Van Morgan is compelled to leave town after he tries to stop his fellow poker players from hanging a man who'd been caught cheating. Then he starts to hear rumors—why are the other players who were at the table being killed off one by one?

5 CARD STUD, 1968

974 Somebody's made a withdrawal

Young orphan Ruby Baker overhears her new guardian, Terry Glass, receive a threatening phone call from a loan shark. She then discovers that a large amount of money is missing from the $4-million trust fund left to her by her deceased parents.

THE GLASS HOUSE, 2001

975 Intense shocker

Kindhearted advertising executive Richard Sullivan is overjoyed when his long-lost cousin Harry and his partner, Connie, arrive on the doorstep. We squirm as we watch Sullivan unreservedly welcome them into his family's home, completely unaware that they have both escaped from a mental institution.

DESPERATE MOTIVE, 1993

976 It was the perfect plan until she refused to be the perfect victim!

A pair of serial kidnappers abducts Abby, the daughter of wealthy Will and Karen Jennings, and conceal her in a woodland hideout. Then they hold Karen, hostage elsewhere, to ensure that her husband pays the ransom. In one scene, while waiting for the money to be paid, Joe Hickey, the mastermind behind the whole plan, makes a move to rape Karen, unaware that she has a knife hidden between her buttocks, and that she is prepared to use it...

TRAPPED, 2002

977 Love held its breath as sudden terror held the stage!

In London's Theatreland, Jonathan Cooper is seen fleeing from the scene of the murder of his mistress's husband. The police are on his trail, so he seeks help from his drama-student friend Eve Gill, who uses a variety of disguises to elude the investigating detective.

STAGE FRIGHT, 1950

978 Who's there?

Carly Bauers is adjusting to her recent blindness when her boyfriend has to go away for a few days, leaving her to her own devices. When the young woman suddenly realizes that she is not alone in her house, her terror is horrifyingly palpable.

NOWHERE IN SIGHT, 2000

979 It's a minefield of a movie

Jean-Paul Belmondo plays ex-gangster Roberto La Rocca, who is in prison with his comrade Xavier Adé (Pierre Vaneck). The two men are in a no-win situation, faced with either serving their time or gaining pardons by volunteering to clear landmines left over from the war. They choose the latter, and we are kept on the edge of our seats in what must be the tensest minefield scene ever captured on film.

A MAN NAMED ROCCA, 1961

980 Meet Hannibal Lecter for the first time

A manhunt is underway for a serial killer who is attacking families in their homes according to a lunar cycle. The FBI asks retired agent Will Graham (Edward Norton) to solve the case, and he visits Hannibal Lecter (Anthony Hopkins) in prison to ask for his help.

Graham: "I don't have much time!"
Lecter: "Oh, but I do! I have oodles!"

RED DRAGON, 2002

981 Time for a nightmare

We follow insomniac Desmond Caine, who sets out into the city during the night to see if a long walk will help clear his mind. During his walk, however, he witnesses a savage murder and he picks up the victim's watch, intending to take it to the police...

DEAD AWAKE, 2001

982 Lend me your ears

In this wonderfully tangled whodunit, a policeman is thrown together with a drama critic to investigate the death of a famous and wealthy actor, who was killed backstage during his niece's Broadway debut. In one gripping scene, the mysterious phantom killer strikes one more time, during a performance of Julius Caesar.

THE PHANTOM OF 42ND STREET, 1945

983 Seeing double

Gina is recovering from the death of her daughter when she sees a girl who looks exactly like her. Stranger still is the fact that the child's mother resembles Gina herself. In one crucial scene, Gina's employer warns her that she may have been drawn into the parallel world of "doppelgängers," and that she could be their next victim.

THE LOOKALIKE, 1991

984 That burning sensation

Young fireman Brian McCaffrey (William Baldwin) is assigned to help investigate a series of mysterious and deadly fires. After fire inspector Donald Rimgale (Robert De Niro) is injured, Brian visits imprisoned arsonist Ronald Bartel (Donald Sutherland), who gives him an insight into the mind of pyromaniacs: "So, whoever is doing this knows that animal well, don't they? They know him real well, but they won't let him loose. They won't let him have any fun. Now, who doesn't love fire?"

BACKDRAFT, 1991

985 In a place this treacherous, what a good spy needs is a spy of his own.

Pierce Brosnan plays a sleazy, unethical spy who meets fellow Brit Geoffrey Rush in the city of Panama. He pressures the poor tailor into spying on his own political clientele, so that Brosnan can send information about their subversive activities back to his superiors in London: "Harry, we're made for each other. You've got the debts, I've got the money. Where's your patriotism?"

THE TAILOR OF PANAMA, 2001

986 A chip off the old block

Roaming adventurer Nick Cochran (Robert Mitchum) is on the run after being convicted of a crime he didn't commit, but that doesn't mean he doesn't have time to pass a few words with the occasional good-looking dame:

Nick Cochran: "You know, you remind me of an old Egyptian girlfriend of mine. The Sphinx."

Margie: "Are you partial to females made of stone?"

MACAO, 1952

987 Vintage British

This comic murder mystery was shot at professional-soccer-team Arsenal's home ground of Highbury in London, and it features many of the players of the time. During a charity match against an amateur team named the Trojans, the center forward, the Trojans' new star player, drops dead—poisoned!

THE ARSENAL STADIUM MYSTERY, 1940

988 The nightmare begins...

Unable to sleep because he cannot understand why his wife has failed to come home, college professor Ed Saxon begins to act irrationally. One of his students comes to the house to see if he is OK, and a minor accident causes her to have a nosebleed. When she departs, she leaves her blood-soaked sweater in his house.

CHASING SLEEP, 2000

989 News from home

Hoping to win a million-dollar prize, a diverse group of young people spend six months living together in an isolated house under constant surveillance via webcams. The only catch is that if one of them goes, they all lose. Then, in the final week, one of the housemates receives a letter from home, which prompts him to try to leave...

MY LITTLE EYE, 2002

990 A rare treat, set in Crete

Young Nikky Ferris (Hayley Mills) meets fellow Englishman Marc Camford (Peter McEnery) while vacationing at the Moon-Spinner hotel on the romantic island of Crete. She falls for him as they dance together to the strains of traditional Greek music. They plan to meet again the next day, but when she leaves Marc alone, he is shot...

THE MOON-SPINNERS, 1964

991 The riddle of life... and death

Shy college student Sara Novak, who is befriended by a comic-bookstore owner with a penchant for riddles, realizes that, with every riddle she solves, someone turns up dead!

NEMESIS GAME, 2003

992 Mystery, levity, horror, and suspense

This hip German suspense thriller is based on an Edgar Wallace novel. A young American girl goes to London to claim an inheritance, and is kidnapped and sent to a strange school for delinquent girls. When Scotland Yard inspectors realize that the school has been the scene of several unsolved murders, they send Inspector Hopkins to investigate.

THE HUNCHBACK OF SOHO, 1966

993 She didn't see that coming

A beautiful blonde woman named Crystal Ball comes seeking a job in a bookstore run by retired mobster Sam Kane, but she is knocked down by a van right outside the store's door. It's later revealed that the amnesia she suffers as a result of the accident has caused her to forget that she is actually an assassin, and that Sam is her target!

SECOND SKIN, 2000

994 It begins with a shriek… it ends with a shot!

College friends Brandon and Philip kill a man just for the "intellectual thrill" of it, and they hide the body in an antique chest in their apartment. They then invite the victim's fiancée, family, and friends to a dinner party, and use the chest as the dining table! Brandon cruelly and arrogantly drops hints about what they have done.
Kenneth: "We're drinking champagne? Is it somebody's birthday?"
Brandon: "You might say it's quite the opposite."

ROPE, 1948

995 She could only run...

During a family business vacation in Amsterdam, Melissa, the mute 10-year-old daughter, sneaks off to the hotel toilet. When she emerges, she can't find her parents, and she strays outside to look for them—just in time to witness the brutal murder of an attorney linked to her father's business deal. The hit man sees her and gives chase...

DO NOT DISTURB, 1999

996 "Are You Lonesome Tonight?"

A flea-pit of a Memphis hotel is the setting for three simultaneous stories. In one, a young widow named Luisa stops at the hotel en route to Italy with her dead husband's body. She wakes in the night to find the ghost of Elvis Presley standing in her room.

MYSTERY TRAIN, 1989

997 "An innocent man has nothing to fear; remember that."

This harrowing Hitchcock movie is based on a true story. Henry Fonda stars as a musician convicted, because of circumstantial evidence, of a robbery he didn't commit. In one scene, he is seen praying in his cell, and his image is superimposed onto the face of the actual criminal, to help us see that he looks absolutely nothing like the guilty man.

THE WRONG MAN, 1956

998 Searing suspense

Georges Campo has a near-fatal car accident. When he recovers consciousness, he doesn't recognize his wife, Christiane, or his psychiatrist friend, Freddie, and his own dog doesn't seem to know him! As George begins to remember his true identity, he secretly stops taking his medication—and that is when he discovers a shocking truth.

DIABOLICALLY YOURS, 1967

999 There goes the "no claims" bonus

An insurance agent arrives for an appointment with a rich, elderly recluse. He is shown into the study by the butler, and he directs his sales pitch to the back of a chair (a plume of cigar smoke has led him to assume that the recluse is seated in it.) He puts his briefcase onto a flat surface, then realizes that it's a coffin—and that his client is in it!

ONE BODY TOO MANY, 1944

1000 Childhood memories

We see a flashback: Three boys playing street hockey are hassled by two plain-clothed cops. The police order one of the boys into their car. As the other boys look on, they drive away, on what is later revealed as a nightmare journey that will scar them all for the rest of their lives.

MYSTIC RIVER, 2003

Index